OUTSOURCING AND CUSTOMER SATISFACTION

OUTSOURCING AND CUSTOMER SATISFACTION

A Study Of PC Help-Desk Services

Dr. Vellore K. Sunder

To order additional copies of this book, contact:
Xlibris Corporation
1-888-795-4274
www.Xlibris.com
Orders@Xlibris.com
82283

CONTENTS

TABLES

FIGURES

DEDICATION

This work is more than a labor of love. It is a testament to the fact that we can be researchers and learners at any age. I dedicate this research study to my beloved wife, Gita, and to my two dear daughters, Punita and Avanija. I am proud of my family.

PREFACE

The term *outsourcing* has become important socially and politically in the United States and other countries around the globe. There seems to be a love-hate relationship with outsourcing. In the United States, outsourcing is blamed for not only loss of jobs in the millions but also for poor customer service. Many sectors of industry and business are impacted by outsourcing: banking, technical help-desk services, health care, insurance, and manufacturing, to name a few.

Focusing on customer services, are we sure outsourced services did not measure up? Did they result in dissatisfied customers? What are some of the determinants of customer satisfaction in outsourced services? How do these compare with nonoutsourced services? What can be done to effect improvements where needed?

This book summarizes my empirical research that sought specifically to determine the factors that impacted customer satisfaction in outsourced services. The personal computing (PC) industry's help-desk service was the focus of my study. The research in its entirety has been published in 2009 as a doctoral dissertation (University of Phoenix).

I was honored to have Dr. Ralph Melaragno as my mentor and chair of the doctoral committee that guided me throughout this research project. Dr. Ralph was very good at nudging me, reviewing my work, and pushing me to the edge of excellence. I admired his patience, tenacity, and passion for precision that guided me to the successful and timely completion of this project. I owe my deepest gratitude to Dr. Ralph.

Dr. Janis McFaul and Dr. William Farrell, as doctoral committee members, pored through nearly two hundred pages of writing and analysis and helped me with valuable insights throughout. My sincere thanks go to Dr. McFaul and Dr. Farrell.

To my dearest wife, Gita, and to my sweet daughters, Punita and Avanija, who have achieved quite a lot in their young lives—a big thank you for supporting me through everything. The three of you have been my loudest cheerleaders.

Nothing could have been achieved without the grace of the Almighty I call Vishnu, who is all-pervasive. To Him I bow with humility, seeking righteous knowledge, strength, and the desire to do good deeds in this world.

CHAPTER 1

In the last several years, the term *outsourcing* has become fairly common among businesses, employees, politicians, and communities. Some like it; some don't. Most of us have experienced one aspect of outsourcing when we call a 1-800 number for help with our credit cards, telephone bills, cable TV services, and software issues. Do we sometimes hear a foreign accent and jump to conclusions? Are we getting excellent service, or is there a need for improvement? This book is the result of a study that sought answers to questions related to quality of perceived outsourced services in one specific segment of business: the help-desk services of the PC industry.

Outsourcing: Importance and Issues

We also hear terms like *offshoring*, *onshoring*, *near sourcing*, and *homesourcing*—all denoting a service performed by someone outside the physical premises of an organization. The use of external agents to perform one or more of organizational activities has been defined as outsourcing (Brooks, 2006). In this book, we will focus on global outsourcing of services (also called *offshoring*). Such outsourcing of services to low-cost countries has significantly increased in the last few years in many sectors.

- Schniederjans and Cao (2006) cite a conference board survey of fifty-two different types of companies in the United States and Europe that indicate that 79% of them outsourced help-desk processes to overseas providers, and that information technology processes were outsourced three times more than any other functional services.

- Deloitte Touche LLP (2005), based on personal interviews with executives from twenty-five large corporations, reported that 70% of the participants had negative experiences with outsourcing and 25% of them wanted to bring back the outsourced services. Negative sentiment toward outsourcing had increased in the literature significantly between the years 2000 and 2004, and the occurrence of negative phrases related to outsourcing increased sevenfold during the same period (Deloitte).

Customer satisfaction with outsourced services is, therefore, an important area for research.

This book summarizes a research study investigating the determinants of customer satisfaction in outsourced help-desk services in the personal computing (PC) industry. Social importance of the research problem, purpose of the study, and the significance of the study to society and business leadership have been discussed in this chapter. Potential independent variables have been identified. Research questions, hypotheses, and possible theoretical frameworks have been presented. Assumptions, scope, limitations, and delimitations conclude the chapter.

Background and Importance of This Study

Outsourcing employs domestic or global subcontractors for the production of goods and services. Global outsourcing of services to low-cost countries significantly increased in the last few years in many sectors like information technology (IT), medical, banking, insurance, and engineering (Alster, 2005; Suuroja, 2003). Jones (2005) estimated that about 3.3 million American IT jobs could move overseas by 2015. Significant among outsourced services are the help-desk services provided by call centers overseas. Barthelemy (2003) estimated that 58% of the organizations would outsource their informational technology services by 2010. These trends indicated that research into customer satisfaction in the outsourced area was timely.

The positives and negatives of outsourcing have been addressed by several research studies from economic, value-chain, strategic, contractual, logistic, or competitiveness perspectives (Doh, 2005; Gottfredson, Puryear, and Phillips, 2005; Koh, Ang, and Straub, 2004; Taylor, 2005). Taylor argues in favor of outsourcing while admitting that there could be some economic disruption as a result, as is inevitable in most productivity enhancement initiatives.

The experiences, attitudes, concerns, and satisfaction levels of US consumers of outsourced services do not seem to have received sufficient attention in research.

- Among the outsourced services affected by concerns of customer satisfaction, 40% was in the business process outsourcing area of which overseas call centers form a part (Deloitte, 2005).
- Scott (2007) reports that poor quality of services and foreign accents made Dell and US Airways pull their call centers from India. Capital One and Conseco shifted a part of their customer support services back to the United States for reasons that included customer dissatisfaction and customer resistance (Alster, 2005).
- American Customer Satisfaction Index (ACSI), published by the University of Michigan, indicated that the service quality in the PC industry was almost 10% below the average of other consumer durables; the lower service quality was attributed, in part, to customer frustrations with PC call centers and to the complex nature of the PC products (as cited in Koprovski, 2006).
- Marshall and Heffes (2005), citing a report by Deloitte Consulting, indicated an undercurrent of customer dissatisfaction in outsourced services.

Customers of traditional domestic sectors, such as laundry, restaurant, hair salons, and similar services have the ability to change their providers often, based on the customers' satisfaction or dissatisfaction with such services. In PC help-desk services, the customer is likely to contact the help-desk telephone number provided by the manufacturer and encounter the quality of service provided without obvious alternate choices. Panther and Farquhar (2004) stress the monitoring of customer satisfaction and an understanding of the reasons of dissatisfaction in order to prevent loss of customers in the service industries. A study of the determinants of customer satisfaction in outsourced PC help-desk services was, therefore, timely and necessary.

The measurement of service quality, as an antecedent to customer satisfaction, was brought into focus with the development of the SERVQUAL tool by Parasuraman, Zeithaml, and Berry (1988). The SERVQUAL tool for analyzing service quality considers customer satisfaction to be a fulfillment of the gap between customer expectations and experiences. Many studies since 1988 have used SERVQUAL (with or without modifications) and other quantitative approaches to assess service quality and customer satisfaction in various service industries like banking, airlines, hospitals, restaurants, and others. From the customer's perspective, assessment of the gap between expectations and experiences may not be difficult in common and repetitive services as in restaurants, laundry, or banking. In the case of help-desk services in the PC industry, the service content may include technical communication and instructions; customers in such cases may not be able to assess the gap between expectations and experiences because of changing technology and unfamiliarity (Chen, 2005). Chapter 2 goes into more details of historical academic research in the area of customer satisfaction.

Research Problem

The general nature of the problem is customer dissatisfaction with perceived outsourced services. We say "perceived" for a reason. The customer calling the help-desk and receiving a response has no real information on where the response originated.

A survey by the Claes Fornell International (CFI) consulting group revealed that PC help-desk service call centers scored the lowest rating of sixty-four among industries studied; the program director of CFI shared the apprehension that many customers with unresolved service issues would switch to another supplier (Mello, 2007). Citing the CFI survey, Mello suggested that while companies might intuitively realize that customer experience with help-desk service centers was important, companies did not understand the finer details of the crucial nature of the relationship. There seemed to be a lack of information on the determinants of customer satisfaction of outsourced help-desk services in the PC industry.

The specific problem was to identify the determinants of customer satisfaction in outsourced PC help-desk services as perceived by owners or users of personal computers in the United States. This study sought a generalizable relationship between several service factors and customer satisfaction in the segment of the industry. An empirical investigation was proposed using a quantitative survey methodology. The general population for the study was of users of personal computer products based in the United States.

The study could benefit the leadership of the personal computing industry in the United States and their overseas service providers in understanding and managing customer satisfaction more effectively, to plan interventions for minimizing crises, and to train their personnel to achieve optimal value addition from outsourcing strategies. The findings of the research study might also provide guidance to business leaders in improving outsourced help-desk services in the banking, health care, insurance, and telecommunication industries since these industries also use such help-desk services.

Purpose of the Research Study

The purpose of the quantitative study was to identify the determinants of customer satisfaction and, in doing so, determine the relationship between several customer service factors and customer satisfaction of perceived outsourced help-desk services in the PC industry. Customer satisfaction and its determinants have been studied extensively in the last twenty years in traditional industries including banking, health care, consumer goods, hospitality, and insurance. There were well-founded conceptual frameworks and extensive statistical methodologies for the study and analysis of customer satisfaction. There was, therefore, no need for an exploratory qualitative study. In the quantitative study, data was collected using e-mail survey questionnaires containing Likert-type scale items that measured certain customer service factors and the perception of customer satisfaction. The dependent variable in the study was customer satisfaction. Based on extensive survey of literature on customer satisfaction, seven independent variables were initially identified for the study. These were (a) responsiveness, (b) reliability, (c) quality of communication, (d) service attitude, (e) empathy, (f) quality of information, and (g) ethics. These seven variables were further divided into forty-two components to enable clarity and unambiguous responses. Quantitative survey methodology was used in the study, drawing on a target of up to two thousand and aimed at getting at least four hundred usable responses from PC users within the United States. The population of PC users in the United States is in the millions. Data was collected using e-mail embedded survey links without limitation on a specific geographic location within the United States.

Significance of This Research Study

Global spending on call centers was estimated at $34 billion in 2006 (Scott, 2007). Bad experiences with call centers had cost $4.5 billion per year in lost customers in Britain alone, according to an executive cited by Scott (2007). Lee (2006) indicated that a lower emphasis on customer service affected Dell Inc.'s revenues negatively in 2005. Beshouri, Farrell, and Umezawa (2005) analyzed outsourcing in the Philippines where more than one hundred thousand people are employed in call centers and reported that subpar practices, corruption, data theft, privacy concerns, and scarce managerial talent were serious issues; any one of these aspects could affect customer satisfaction.

Bharadwaj and Roggeveen (2008) examined customer appraisals of offshore and onshore call-center services for one specific PC services company and concluded that there was a lower level of customer appraisal for offshored services. The authors attribute the result to the homophily (like attracts like) concept. Bharadwaj and Roggeveen have recommended detailed research studies to include factors other than geographic location and to investigate ways to improve offshored services.

Fairell, Kaka, and Stürze (2005) cited research by McKinsey Global Institute that indicated poor English communication skills and strong accents with some of the Indian call-center service providers, forcing firms to shift their call-center services to other low-cost countries. While assessing local socio-political conditions in such countries is not the purpose of the research, a study of customer satisfaction related to call-center services could bring out areas where training interventions could be made with the goal of improving customer satisfaction. The research study focused on the PC help-desk services industry to study the determinants of customer satisfaction.

Significance to Business Leadership

The impact of customer satisfaction on businesses has been studied by several researchers.

- Anderson, Fornell, and Mazvancheryl (2004) studied two hundred Fortune 500 firms and concluded that a 1% improvement in the ACSI could lead to an increase of $240 million in the market value of a firm.

- Also based on their studies of ACSI, Gruca and Rego (2005) suggested that a single point increase in ACSI produced an increase of $55 million in a firm's net operational cash flow.
- Gupta and Zeithaml (2006) discussed several research studies and made an empirical generalization that improvement in customer satisfaction had a significant and positive impact on the financial performance of firms. Gupta and Zeithaml indicated that a 1% drop in the satisfaction rating resulted in about a 5% drop in the return on investment.

The linkage of long-term success of business and firm profitability to customer satisfaction has been established by many researchers.

- Lee and Hwan (2005) studied the relationship of corporate profitability in Taiwanese firms and concluded that customer satisfaction was indeed an antecedent to profitability.
- Yu (2007) studied the banking industry in Taiwan and empirically validated the relationship between customer satisfaction, repurchase intention, and the firm's reputation. Yu also established a direct link between customer satisfaction and profitability.
- Yeung and Ennew (2000) used the data from the ACSI and evaluated the relationship between **customer** satisfaction and measures of **financial performance**. Their results suggested that improved customer satisfaction did have a positive impact on financial results.
- Smith and Wright (2004) studied customer satisfaction and loyalty in the PC industry and concluded that high customer loyalty resulted in competitive advantage for manufacturers.

A study of determinants of customer satisfaction is, therefore, important to business leaders in achieving both short-term and long-term corporate objectives.

Thus, in managing customer relationships in the twenty-first century, a leader's responsibility will be to increase customer satisfaction through the entire organization by monitoring every interaction with the customer and by enhancing customer value. Payne and Frow (2005) developed a conceptual framework for customer relationship management (CRM) that helps broaden the understanding of CRM and its role in enhancing customer value and, as a result, shareholder value. Payne and Frow have pointed out that customer satisfaction, an integral part of the value creation process and an important metric, reached only 36% of the board of directors as a concern. Identifying determinants of customer satisfaction (and, thus, actionable items) may bring a higher degree of attention from the leadership and help improve firm value as discussed earlier.

Discussing the broader firm strategy, organizational alignment, and technology as part of customer relationship management, Roberts, Liu, and Hazard (2005) considered customer satisfaction as one of three objectives—loyalty and retention being the other two. Luo and Bhattacharya (2006) examined the linkages between corporate social responsibility (CSR), customer satisfaction, and market value creation; achieving customer satisfaction was determined to be one of the ways of realizing the financial returns and increasing the market value crucial to business leaders.

Given the aforementioned examples from the United States and from other countries of linkages between customer satisfaction, profitability, shareholder value, competitive advantage, customer retention, and long-term business success, the significance of the study to leadership could be summarized in the following terms:

1. The study brought out specific determinants of customer satisfaction in perceived outsourced help-desk services.
2. The study provided guidelines to leadership on training the service providers in addressing cultural, language, and communication barriers.
3. Satisfied customers also influence employee attitudes and performance (Wells, 2007).
4. Leaders could expect higher efficiencies in future advertising and promotional expenditure because of improved customer satisfaction (Luo and Homburg, 2007).
5. Future studies based on suggested areas of research might provide guidelines to leaders for developing customer-satisfaction-based metrics to assess customer retention and lifetime value in outsourced service situations (Gupta and Zeithaml, 2006).
6. Leadership could address causes of dissatisfaction and possibly achieve higher long-term customer retention through appropriate interventions (Radcliffe and Simpson, 2008).
7. Customer satisfaction has been known to have a direct impact on the corporation's reputation and image (Chun, 2005). The research study could help leaders to manage corporate reputation and image better by managing customer satisfaction.

Tam (2004) developed an integral model linking customer satisfaction, service quality, and perceived value; the study concluded that customer satisfaction and perceived value significantly influenced postpurchase behavior represented by future recommendations and purchase intentions. Thus, as a part of successful customer relationship management, measurement and analysis of customer satisfaction were important to the leaders of organizations.

Nature of the Study

This quantitative study identified the determinants of customer satisfaction in outsourced PC help-desk services as perceived by the customers. Customer satisfaction in manufacturing industries and traditional service industries like banking, insurance, hospitals, travel, restaurant, and others had been studied extensively for more than fifteen years. Several methodologies have been used in customer-satisfaction research (see for example, Chan and Ibrahim, 2004; Cronin and Taylor, 1992; Jeyapaul, Shahabudeen, and Krishnaiah, 2005; Parasuraman et al., 1988).

In outsourced PC help-desk services, there is a combination of technical and communication issues at both ends; it is not known whether the customer will be able to express expectations or judge the deficiencies immediately. In the current study of customer satisfaction in help-desk services, there is thus a need to follow a combinatorial approach, considering factors that represent technical competence, communication competence, service attitude, service behavior, as well as the effects of cultural dimensions that influence these variables. Based on extensive review of literature, seven independent variable constructs were examined for the quantitative study. Each of these independent variable constructs was made up of several components. The variables and their forty-two components have been listed in table 1.

In addition to independent variables and their components described in table 1, the design of the survey instrument took into account additional demographic and intervening variables. These have been listed in table 2.

Rationale for Choice of Methodology and Design

A search of various article databases revealed that there was a considerable amount of literature on customer satisfaction although customer satisfaction in outsourced PC help-desk services had not yet been investigated. There was, thus, a body of well-developed definitions of concepts and constructs in the general field of customer satisfaction, customer relationship, and leadership interventions. There were also several models that had seen applications in banking, health care, tourism, and other services (e.g., Barsky and Nash, 2003; Lee and Hwan, 2005; Sharma and Ojha, 2004). There seemed to be sufficient qualitative and quantitative foundation available for use in the current study.

Table 1
Potential Independent Variables and Their Components

Variable	Definitions and components
Responsiveness	Responsiveness is defined as a willingness to help, accompanied by courtesy, quick response, and a speedy resolution of the customer's concerns—four components (Parasuraman et al., 1988; Parasuraman, Zeithaml, and Malhotra, 2005).
Reliability	Reliability is defined by a combination of five components: dependability, technical competence, availability on call, error-free instruction, and sincerity (Parasuraman et al., 1988; Parasuraman et al., 2005).
Quality of communication	Quality of communication is a construct based on a combination of fifteen concepts: acceptable speed of delivery of speech, accent, intonation, clarity of pronunciation, clarity of instruction, explanation, comprehensibility by customer, fluency in English, vocabulary, grammar, vocal intensity, pauses, ability to understand customer, live guidance through process, and follow-through (Boshoff and Staude, 2003; Matsuura, Chiba, and Fujieda, 1999).

Table 1 *continued*

Variable	Definitions and components
Service attitude	The construct of service attitude has the four components of concern for the customer, civility, congeniality, genuineness in assisting the customer. It is a predisposition of the service provider even before the customer discusses the service issue at hand (Winsted, 2000).
Empathy	Empathy is a set of expressed attitudes that covers six aspects: expressions of caring remarks, consideration for customer's time and urgency, ability to listen patiently, trustworthiness, friendliness, and attentiveness (Parasuraman et al., 1988).
Quality of information	Quality of information is defined as a combination of four concepts: accuracy, timeliness, relevance, and the ease of use of information given to the customer (Kuo, Lu, Huang, and Wu, 2005).
Ethics	Ethics in a service encounter combines the four expectations of security, privacy, nondeception, and a fulfillment of promise (Roman, 2007).

Table 2
Potential Intervening Variables

INT-1	Gender	Male/Female
INT-2	Make of PC	Apple/Dell/Gateway/HP/IBM/Sony/Toshiba/Other
INT-3	When was the service call made	3 months/More than 3 months/Do not remember
INT-4	Perceived source of service	Domestic/Offshore

Edmondson and McManus (2007) categorized management field research into three categories—nascent, intermediate, and mature studies—and discussed methodological fit for each of these. While prior theory and research were undeveloped or being developed in the case of nascent and intermediate studies, mature studies had well-established theories, concepts, and constructs. The goals of research in nascent and intermediate studies were either exploratory or pattern seeking, whereas mature studies tested hypotheses in new scenarios based heavily on established constructs and theories. Mature studies had been described as those that test theory-driven hypotheses, employ quantitative survey methodologies that yield quantitative results, and contributed to increased and more precise quantitative understanding of the issue at hand.

Given the knowledge base of published research and well-defined variables in the field of customer satisfaction, research into the identification of determinants of customer satisfaction could be classified as mature research and, thus, qualified for a quantitative approach. Recognizing the nature of help-desk services that use telecommunication (telephone and Internet) channels, a firsthand qualitative exploratory observation of hundreds of service encounters followed by customer interviews would not be necessary, nor would it be an appropriate or practical choice in a study of customer satisfaction in the PC industry.

This research study was quantitative, drawing upon some of the established concepts and constructs, supplemented by additional concepts drawn from the areas of global communication and culture. Adapting the concepts and constructs derived from several customer service variables indicated in tables 1 and 2, a quantitative survey was conducted using a Likert-type questionnaire to investigate the relationship between the variables and customer satisfaction of outsourced help-desk services in the PC industry. A questionnaire-based survey was expected to eliminate biases arising out of qualitative interviews. The potential to collect and analyze sizeable data, availability of widely accepted statistical tools, and larger samples made the quantitative design more suitable and was instrumental in greater accuracy in identifying the significant independent variables and their relationships to customer satisfaction.

Likert and Likert-type scales have been widely used for research in the area of customer satisfaction. Some academicians were of the opinion that Likert and Likert-type surveys produce ordinal data and should, therefore, be analyzed only by nonparametric statistical methodologies (Jamieson, 2004). Despite this, hundreds of research studies in the area of customer satisfaction, for all practical purposes, considered Likert survey data as interval data and proceeded to analyze the data with parametric methods. Allen and Rao (2000) made an argument that establishing anchors only for the scale end points (as opposed to labeling all the scale points) would produce interval data that can be analyzed through parametric analysis.

A Likert-type scale with anchors established only at the ends was used in the study. As stated by Allen and Rao (2000), in such a scale anchored only at the ends, a score of four given by a respondent could reasonably be assumed to be double in magnitude of a score represented by two on the same scale. Analysis of survey data was done using confirmatory factor analysis and univariate multiple regression in order to identify determinants of customer satisfaction and to assess the degree, direction, and sensitivity of relationship between the independent variables and customer satisfaction. Factor analysis and regression helped achieve the following outcomes:

1. A reduction in the number of components of variables.
2. Identification of the variables that have a significant impact on customer satisfaction.
3. An understanding of the relationship of each of the independent variables with customer satisfaction, the dependent variable, in respect of degree, direction, and sensitivity.

Research Questions and Hypotheses

The dependent variable in this study was customer satisfaction. Based on various definitions of customer satisfaction found in literature (e.g., Bartikowski, Barthelemy, and Llosa, 2004; Garbarino and Johnson, 1999) and pursuant to the stated problem and purpose of the research study, the following working definition of customer satisfaction was used in the study: *Customer satisfaction* was defined as a postservice evaluative judgment of a service encounter with a remote provider based on an assessment of the performance of various attributes that constitute that service. Customer satisfaction itself was the antecedent of other dependant variables such as customer loyalty, trust, and value (Agustin and Singh, 2005). The present study will limit itself to studying customer satisfaction.

The effect and direction of influence, if any, of each of the variables were analyzed in the study. A two-tail test was used in testing hypotheses at 95% confidence level. Based on the seven variables chosen for the study, the research questions and hypotheses initially proposed were as follows:

RQ 1: What effect does quality of responsiveness have on customer satisfaction in outsourced help-desk situations?

H_0: Quality of responsiveness has no effect on customer satisfaction in outsourced help-desk situations.

H_A: Quality of responsiveness has an effect on customer satisfaction in outsourced help-desk situations.

RQ 2: What effect does reliability of the service provider have on customer satisfaction in outsourced help-desk situations?

H_0: Reliability of the service provider has no effect on customer satisfaction in outsourced help-desk situations.

H_A: Reliability of the service provider has an effect on customer satisfaction in outsourced help-desk situations.

RQ 3: What effect does quality of communication have on customer satisfaction in outsourced help-desk situations?

H_0: Quality of communication has no effect on customer satisfaction in outsourced help-desk situations.

H_A: Quality of communication has an effect on customer satisfaction in outsourced help-desk situations.

RQ 4: What effect does attitude of the service provider have on customer satisfaction in outsourced help-desk situations?

H_0: Attitude of the service provider has no effect on customer satisfaction in outsourced help-desk situations.

H_A: Attitude of the service provider has an effect on customer satisfaction in outsourced help-desk situations.

RQ 5: What effect does empathy of the service provider have on customer satisfaction in outsourced help-desk situations?

H_0:   Empathy of the service provider has no effect on customer satisfaction in outsourced help-desk situations.

H_A: Empathy of the service provider has an effect on customer satisfaction in outsourced help-desk situations.

RQ 6:   What effect does quality of information given by the service provider have on customer satisfaction in outsourced help-desk situations?

H_0:   Quality of information given by the service provider has no effect on customer satisfaction in outsourced help-desk situations.

H_A: Quality of information given by the service provider has an effect on customer satisfaction in outsourced help-desk situations.

RQ 7:   What effect do ethics of the service provider have on customer satisfaction in outsourced help-desk situations?

H_0:   Ethics of the service provider has no effect on customer satisfaction in outsourced help-desk situations.

H_A: Ethics of the service provider has an effect on customer satisfaction in outsourced help-desk situations.

In addition to providing a means of confirming or rejecting the null hypothesis in each of seven cases, the survey was expected to provide insights into the degree of impact of the independent variables on customer satisfaction.

Conceptual Frameworks

Outsourcing of services had been regarded as a value-chain activity with firms trying to achieve cost advantages at acceptable quality levels (Gottfredson, Puryear, and Phillips, 2005). On the other hand, customer satisfaction, in the case of outsourced services, very much would become a part of the customer relationship management and was linked to long-term business success and competitive advantage (see for example Luo and

Bhattacharya, 2006; Payne and Frow, 2005; Smith and Wright, 2004). A funnel approach shown in figure 1 is the theoretical area under which the study belonged:

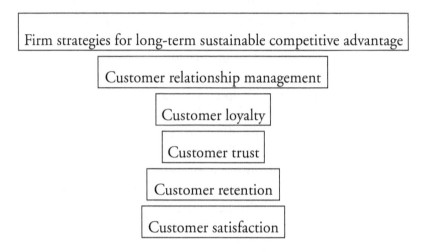

Figure 1. Customer satisfaction leading to long-term sustainable competitive advantage

The measurement of customer satisfaction had been approached from several conceptual angles. Service quality had been linked to customer satisfaction by several researchers. While Bitner (1990) considered customer satisfaction as the antecedent of service quality, later research by Cronin and Taylor (1992) concluded that service quality was the antecedent of customer satisfaction. A widely used approach was the recognition of service quality as an antecedent of customer satisfaction. Customer perceptions of various service-quality parameters were therefore considered necessary for the measurement of CS. A few such models have been described in the following sections.

The Gap-Analysis Framework

The measurement of service quality (as an antecedent to customer satisfaction) was brought into focus with the development of the SERVQUAL tool by Parasuraman et al. (1988). The gap-analysis approach used by SERVQUAL aimed to measure the difference between the expectation of service quality from the best provider and the perceived service quality from the current provider. The SERVQUAL used five categories of service quality—responsiveness, reliability, empathy, tangible, and assurance. These five categories were further divided into two sets of twenty-two variables that were then measured. The availability of the SERVQUAL tool had made it possible to be used in several studies.

The shortcomings of SERVQUAL had been pointed out by several authors (e.g., Buttle, 1996; Sureshchandar, Rajendran, and Kamalanabhan, 2001; van Dyke, Kappelman, Leon, and Prybutok, 1997). Among the conceptual difficulties pointed out were the operationalization of perceived service quality as a gap score and the ambiguity of the expectations construct. In the case of PC help-desk services (unlike, for example, traditional and repeated services like laundry, hair salons, restaurants, and banks), technological aspects were involved; customers might not know what to expect. Thus, customers might not be able to assess gaps between expectations and service rendered. Suuroja (2003) had analyzed various studies on service quality that proved that the quality of service should be assessed by a direct evaluation of service attributes and not as a gap from expectations. Gap-analysis approach, in the case of PC help-desk services, might not be the most appropriate.

Performance-Only Framework

Cronin and Taylor (1992) pointed out deficiencies in SERVQUAL and suggested that the measurement of gap (and disconfirmation thereof) had no theoretical basis. An alternative approach based on the measurement of service performance (SERVPERF) with a twenty-one-item scale was suggested. Cronin and Taylor argued that the SERVPERF model took better cognizance of the customer's attitudes, explained the variations in service quality better, and was a better predictor of purchase intentions. SERVPERF had also been criticized as being too generic to indicate industry-specific dimensions of service quality (Cunningham, Young, and Lee, 2002).

Service Quality Loss Framework

Another approach to measuring SQ was to measure a concept called service quality loss. Taguchi and Clausing introduced the loss-function method in 1990 primarily for the manufacturing industry based on the concept that any variability in service introduces a cost, called the Taguchi loss. The Taguchi method had been criticized as being too restrictive as it was based on the single-response model (Liao, 2003). Later, researchers had proposed modified loss-function approaches using multiresponse models (Chan and Ibrahim, 2004; Jeyapaul et al., 2005). The Taguchi loss model was more suited to manufacturing and process control since a measure of variability over time was required.

Motivation-Hygiene Framework

Drawing from the well-known Herzberg motivation-hygiene theories, Kano, in 1974, proposed the motivation-hygiene theory of quality considering five classes of quality based on satisfaction-dissatisfaction and functional-dysfunctional classification. Yang (2005) refined the Kano model by subdividing the classes further. Matzler, Fuchs, and Schubert (2004) used the Kano approach coupled with regression analysis to study employee satisfaction. Kano's model had been combined with SERVQUAL by Chen and Lee (2006) to study dormitory service quality in a university setting.

A Conceptual Model for the Current Study

The current study considered some of the constructs—like responsiveness, reliability, and empathy—that have been used as variables in several studies of customer satisfaction in tangible and intangible goods. Outsourced help-desk services brought in additional aspects of global cultures and communication. Kuo et al. (2005) studied the importance of the variable of quality of information in their research of Web portals. Customer dissatisfaction indications with locally and globally outsourced services were pointing in the area of communication (see Fornell cited in Koprovski, 2006). Variables that impacted communication in the customer-provider interface had been studied by Boshoff and Staude (2003) and Matsuura, Chiba, and Fujieda (1999). Components of communication (see table 1) were therefore included as possible antecedents to customer satisfaction in outsourced services.

Barger and Grandey (2006), analyzing local service encounters (as different from online or on-telephone encounters), concluded that there was evidence to support that service with a smile resulted in higher perception of service quality and a higher level of customer satisfaction. Intensity of smile, pre-encounter smile, and postencounter smile were significant influencers of customer satisfaction. Smile was an indication of attitude and empathy. In the context of a remote service provider, as in outsourced PC help-desk services, there was a need to examine if variables like service attitude or empathy could, in effect, achieve an equivalent of an *online smile*. Empathy and attitude, therefore, were included as independent variables.

Chen (2005) observed that many service encounters in the age of technology were in the nature of self-service technology (SST) encounters where the customer produced service without the direct interpersonal involvement of a service employee. Chen concluded that the determinants of customer satisfaction in the SST and interpersonal encounters are different. Service encounters in the PC help-desk services often had an element of SST at the customer's end that was impacted by the quality of communication and information.

Suuroja (2003), after an analysis of various service-related research studies, indicated that standardization of service attributes across industries had not been fruitful, and there was a need for a customized approach in different service sectors. Derived from these arguments and findings, a conceptual model was proposed in figure 2 for the PC help-desk services sector. Shaded boxes represented the variables under study.

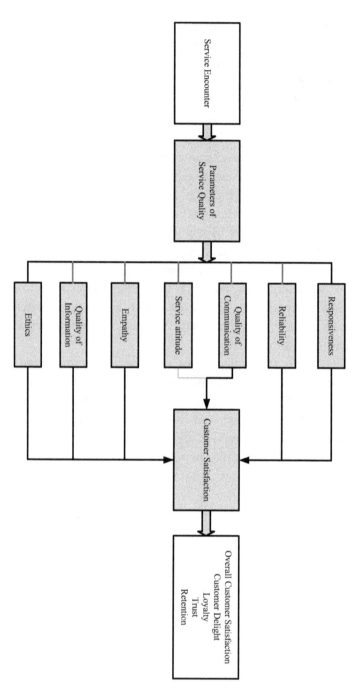

Figure 2. A conceptual framework showing customer satisfaction
and the seven independent variables

Operational Definitions of Terms

The broader operational definitions of *outsourcing, service encounter, service quality, customer satisfaction,* and other terms have been given in the section. Definitions of potential independent variables in terms of their components have been given in table 1 with supporting citations.

Outsourcing. Outsourcing has been defined as the use of external agents to perform one or more of organizational activities (Brooks, 2006). In the research study, the term *outsourcing* was used to indicate both domestic and global outsourcing (called offshoring). However, the variables used for data collection were expected to assist in delineating factors that are specific to customer satisfaction related to global outsourcing.

Help-desk services. Help-desk services in the study were services rendered telephonically in response to a telephonic request initiated by the customers. There could be a conversation with or without a simultaneous online interface.

Personal computing industry. Personal computing (synonymous in the study with personal computers) industry referred to manufacturers, suppliers, and distributors of desktop and laptop computers.

Customers. Individual users of personal computers who received services from outsourced help-desk services based on their individual service requests. Such customers might not be the owners of personal computers and laptops.

Service quality. Service quality was defined in the study as a set of judgments of various factors experienced during the service encounter. The seven independent variables and their components (table 1) were representative of such factors.

Customer satisfaction. Customer satisfaction was defined in the study, closely following the definition given by Oliver (1980), as a "postservice evaluative judgment of a service encounter resulting in a pleasurable end-state, based on a combined assessment of the performance of service factors that constituted that service." The preceding definition of customer satisfaction was operationalized based on an analysis of the survey responses received.

Operational Definitions of Independent Variables

There are seven independent variable constructs that were identified for the study. Their operational definitions have been shown in table 1.

Assumptions

In conducting the research study through survey questionnaires, a fundamental assumption was that the respondents would provide truthful responses to the best of their knowledge. Survey questionnaires, by their very nature, depend on the psychological phenomenon of incident recall. An assumption was made that respondents would be willing to provide complete information requested in the survey instrument based on incident recall.

Another assumption was that there was no difference in the quality of information provided by the respondents whether Internet or e-mail modality was used to collect survey responses. Quality of communication was a potential variable that is being studied. An assumption here was that customers who sought and received help-desk services could understand basic instructions and could communicate in the English language over telephone.

The respondents in the survey might have belonged to different cultures, ethnicities, and may speak a variety of languages in addition to English, although all of them were US residents. The heterogeneity of respondents in terms of culture or ethnicity was assumed to have no impact on the respondents' judgments of service quality and satisfaction.

Another aspect of customer heterogeneity was the level of product knowledge of each respondent. Product knowledge, being a characteristic of the customer, could vary from customer to customer as well as from product to product. Some influence of product knowledge might become evident in customers' ability to understand and respond to technical communication or instruction. The influence of product knowledge would likely be seen in customers' judgment of the variable "quality of communication." The independent variables in the study focused on service factors that influenced customer satisfaction. Customer product knowledge as a separate intervening variable was therefore not considered in the study.

There have been several state initiatives in the United States aimed at using only local help-desk services located within the United States (Schultz, 2006). These actions from the states could either encourage or require that state contractors not procure call-center services offshore. So far, such legislation proposals have been limited in scope to state contracts and state contractors. Since these initiatives from the states did not cover most individual owners of PCs, the effect of such legislation was assumed not to influence the study of customer satisfaction in PC help-desk services or the validity of findings that might emanate from the research study.

Scope, Limitations, and Delimitations

Scope

The outsourcing phenomenon has pervaded many service sectors like insurance, banking, health care, manufactured products, medical transcriptions, engineering design services, and others. The study focused on the PC help-desk services that were outsourced locally or globally. Research was based on data collected through questionnaires in e-mailed surveys. A target sample of up to two thousand customers was expected to be surveyed to generate no less than four hundred usable responses. While the psychological nature of customer satisfaction might be similar across industries, the factors that determine customer satisfaction were expected to be different in different types of industries. For example, help-desk services in the banking or insurance industry might not involve the level of technical knowledge or skill that the PC help-desk services require on the part of the provider or receiver of such services. Data analyses using factor analysis and univariate multiple regression were used in the extraction of factors that significantly influenced customer satisfaction in outsourced PC help-desk services.

Limitations

Since a quantitative survey instrument was employed, there was a limitation on how many questions a respondent may be asked without the respondent becoming disinterested. The second limitation was that the accuracy of data provided by the respondents depended on the capability of the respondent to recall service-encounter experiences. These limitations could be inherent in any customer satisfaction survey, but the effects of these limitations were sought to be minimized through a proper design of the survey instrument. An important aspect of the survey was that the determination of the perceived source of help-desk services (local or foreign) would be based on the judgment of the respondents. The respondent was assumed to give accurate and sincere responses.

The survey questionnaire was a Likert-type instrument. There have been differing academic opinions on whether parametric statistical tests and inferences were applicable in the analysis of Likert-type questions

(Clason and Dormody, 1994; Gardner and Martin, 2007; Jamieson, 2004). The objections have revolved around three points: (a) ordinal nature of Likert-type data, (b) non-normality of Likert-type data, and (c) differences in respondents' qualitative judgment of degrees of separation between scale points.

Notwithstanding these objections, parametric tests have been widely used on Likert-type data by hundreds of researchers. There were suggestions that a large sample size, more questions, a wider scale of response categories, and establishment of anchors only for the scale end points might bring in conditions that supported parametric tests (Allen and Rao, 2000; Clason and Dormody, 1994; Lubke and Muthen, 2004).

Delimitations and Generalizability

At least four hundred usable responses were to be collected, but the study would not impose any limitation on the number of responses received beyond four hundred. The independent variables indicated in earlier sections of the study were generic in nature, although these variables were being studied in the context of the PC industry. The findings might be generalizable in similar help-desk services across other industries with or without modifications.

Chapter Summary

Outsourcing of services have continued to increase significantly in recent years, particularly in the information technology sector. Global outsourcing of services (also called offshoring) to low-cost countries has significantly increased in the last few years in many sectors. Yet there have been concerns about the quality of outsourced services at both the customer level and leadership level. A survey by the CFI consulting group revealed that the PC help-desk service call centers scored the lowest rating of sixty-four among industries studied (as cited in Mello, 2007). Using quantitative survey methodology, seven variables that influence customer satisfaction in the segment of the PC industry were examined in the research study. Significance of the study, research hypotheses, operating definitions, assumptions, and limitations were addressed in the chapter.

The study was expected to benefit the leadership of PC companies in improving customer satisfaction in outsourced services, in planning interventions for minimizing crises, and in training their personnel to achieve optimal value addition from the help-desk services. The literature review in the next chapter has gone into the historical review of research on customer satisfaction, definitions of various independent variables, relative merits of various methodologies, and contrarian points of view.

CHAPTER 2

LITERATURE REVIEW

The details described in the previous chapter require that the literature review deal with various aspects of customer satisfaction as related to help-desk services specific to the personal computing (PC) industry. Customer satisfaction as a management strategy has been researched for more than two decades. Other related constructs like customer loyalty, service quality, service encounters, customer retention, customer delight, and customer relationship management have also entered the research discussions. Among these related constructs, service quality and its components will be discussed as antecedents of customer satisfaction, the dependent variable. Constructs such as customer retention and customer relationship management will be reviewed as leadership objectives in the long run.

The literature review begins with a general perspective on the status and trends in outsourcing of services and its place in a firm's value-chain strategy, followed by a brief review of cross-cultural issues. Next is a discussion of the importance of customer satisfaction to firm strategy and leadership. Gaps in literature with respect to customer-satisfaction studies in the PC help-desk service industry are highlighted.

A search of article databases shows that there are thousands of research articles on customer satisfaction spread over more than fifteen years and covering many industrial and service sectors. Customer satisfaction in outsourced PC help-desk services has not been studied until this study was published in 2009. The literature review covers about 158 publications between 1988 and 2008. In addition to understanding the academic treatment of customer satisfaction as a concept and understanding the determinants of customer satisfaction in various industries, various analytical methodologies will be examined in the chapter. Both supportive and contrarian points of view have been examined.

Narrowing the focus from general to the specific, the literature review begins with a historical overview of research on customer satisfaction and its determinants in different types of industries. Germinal research and methodologies employed in other research studies are examined. A definition of customer satisfaction is given based on a discussion of several constructs. A group of independent variables and intervening variables will be identified and discussed.

The use of external agents to perform one or more organizational activities has been defined as *outsourcing* (Brooks, 2006). Without going into the merits of whether outsourcing of any type is good or bad, the review offers proof that outsourcing and offshoring of services globally will continue to grow (Barthelemy, 2003). The focus of the review will be literature related to customer satisfaction in services, potential antecedents to customer satisfaction, methodologies for measurement of customer satisfaction, leadership implications, and multicultural factors influencing customer satisfaction.

Historical Overview

More than forty years ago, Theodore Levitt brought out the strategic differences between selling and marketing and voiced a strong case for marketing orientation in his classic work *Marketing Myopia* (Bailey, 2006). Levitt suggested that the entire organization must be viewed as a customer-creating and customer-satisfying organism. In the years following, literature focused on customer—or market-driven strategies. The well-known needs hierarchy theory of Maslow provided further support to the assessment of customer needs and their satisfaction. Forty years afterward, Chiu and Lin (2004) have tried to provide a linkage between the needs theory and customer satisfaction in their study of service quality measurement using Maslow's framework.

Historical Perspectives on Customer Satisfaction

Oliver (1980) provided an empirical basis for understanding the cognitive model of the antecedents and consequences of satisfaction decisions made by the consumer. Oliver introduced the concepts of expectation-satisfaction gap and confirmed that customer satisfaction had a higher magnitude of impact on a customer's postattitude and postintentions. Customer satisfaction was regarded as the precursor of long-term customer retention, loyalty, and positive consumer behavior. Customer satisfaction continues to be studied in all facets of manufacturing and service industries.

The antecedents of customer satisfaction then engaged the researchers. Parasuraman et al. (1988) brought into focus the measurement of service quality as an antecedent to customer satisfaction with the development of the SERVQUAL tool. Cronin and Taylor (1992) provided a different approach based on the assessment of performance only and not gaps. Many studies since 1988 have used SERVQUAL and SERVPERF, with or without modifications, to assess service quality and customer satisfaction in various service industries like banking, airlines, hospitals, Web services, and others. Limitations of and objections to SERVQUAL were mentioned in chapter 1.

At the onset of the twenty-first century, customer satisfaction came to be considered within the larger context of customer relationship management (CRM). Payne and Frow (2005) developed a conceptual framework for CRM in enhancing customer value and, shareholder value; five cross-functional strategies were identified. Horn, Feinberg, and Salvendy (2005) and Shah and Murtaza (2005) studied customer satisfaction within the CRM framework in e-businesses and Web-based services. Consumer dissatisfaction responses and complaint behavior were analyzed by Crie (2003) who proposed an integrated framework of the various theories of complaint behavior.

Approaches to Definition and Measurement of Customer Satisfaction

Definitions of customer satisfaction and potential antecedent variables are explored in the following sections, and a working definition of customer satisfaction is advanced. Literature on various methodologies available for measurement of the variables is examined. An appropriate choice of methodology is briefly discussed.

Definitions of Customer Satisfaction

People may generally understand the meanings of phrases customer satisfaction and satisfied customer from their individual perspectives.

Leaders of industry, managers, and researchers have to deconstruct these phrases to guide businesses to be effective and efficient in achieving customer retention in the end. It was necessary, therefore, to examine the definitions of customer satisfaction in academic research to help arrive at a working definition for the current study of PC help-desk services.

Customer satisfaction has been defined as the degree of fulfillment of some need, desire, goal, or other pleasurable end state that results from a specific exchange transaction between the consumer and a firm (Oliver and Rust, 1997). Zeithmal and Bitner (2003) gave a slightly different definition: "Satisfaction is the consumer fulfillment response. It is a judgment that a product or service feature, or the product or service itself, provides a pleasurable level of consumption-related fulfillment" (p. 86). Citing Derrow, CEO of a manufacturing company, Griffiths (2006) gave a definition of customer satisfaction, differentiating satisfaction from loyalty: "Satisfaction is defined by what people say; loyalty is defined by what they do" (p. 34).

Literature identifies two types of customer satisfaction: transaction-specific satisfaction and overall satisfaction. Customer satisfaction arising out of a single service transaction is referred to as transaction-specific customer satisfaction. In addition to such transaction-specific customer satisfaction, Bolton (as cited in Johnson, Garbarino, and Sivadas, 2006) proposed the construct of a continually updated cumulative satisfaction that could be called overall satisfaction. A single item of overall or global satisfaction measure has been shown to be useful in predicting overall behaviors and attitudes (Oliver, 1997). Such overall satisfaction measurements may be useful in compiling and comparing intraindustry indices like ACSI (Koprovski, 2006) and in assessing customer loyalty over time (Zulganef, 2006), but they do not give sufficient and detailed pointers to the leaders and managers of businesses in improving specific industries like the PC help-desk services. Transaction-specific customer satisfaction measurements (as different from overall satisfaction measurements) yield diagnostic information about various service factors in specific transactions (Chatterjee and Chatterjee, 2005). The present cross-sectional study of customer satisfaction in outsourced PC help-desk services will focus on transaction-specific customer satisfaction. All further references to customer satisfaction in the study would mean transaction-specific customer satisfaction.

Some Aspects of Measurement of Customer Satisfaction

The SERVQUAL tool for analyzing service quality considered customer satisfaction to be a fulfillment of the gap, also referred to as disconfirmation of gap, between customer expectations and experiences. McEwen (2004) and Bartikowski, Barthelemy, and Llosa (2004) have cited several studies and have arrived at a definition of customer satisfaction as an overall assessment of the performance of various attributes of a product or a service. Meyer and Schwager (2007) have suggested that customer satisfaction was made of the net of good and bad experiences and that customer satisfaction reflected the bridging of the gap between expectations and experiences; the concept closely mirrors the SERVQUAL concept. Oliver (1997) analyzed behavioral perspectives and suggested customer satisfaction as the occurrence of positive disconfirmation of expectancies similar to those proposed in the SERVQUAL approach. Douglas and Fredendall (2004) considered customer satisfaction as the degree to which customers perceived their needs as being met.

In the current study, customer satisfaction is defined as "a postservice evaluative judgment of a service encounter resulting in a pleasurable end-state, based on a combined assessment of the performance of service factors that constituted that service." The preceding definition of customer satisfaction will be operationalized based on an analysis of the survey responses received.

Service Encounters and Customer Satisfaction

Service encounters are contacts between a customer and an employee of the service firm. Numerous researchers have examined the relationship between service encounters and customer satisfaction. Some are highlighted below:

1. Economidou-Kogetsidis (2005) defined service encounters as conversations for a transactional exchange, which mostly involved some sort of request. In help-desk services, calling a telephone number by a customer would constitute such a request and trigger a service encounter.
2. Service encounters are also referred to as "moments of truth" in customer service (Beaujean, Davidson, and Madge, 2006).

3. Service encounters could result in transaction-specific customer satisfaction or dissatisfaction. Jones, Mak, and Sim (2007), in their study of customer satisfaction in the hotel industry, indicates that intangible aspects of service encounter had greater weight than certain tangibles in customers' perception of service quality.

4. Massad, Heckman, and Crowston (2006) investigated service encounters and customer satisfaction in the online retailing industry and found that the characteristics and behaviors of **customer**-contact employees played an important role in online **service encounters.** The study revealed that unsatisfactory incidents increased as **service encounters** moved from a bricks-and-mortar environment to an **electronic** context.

5. Bennington, Cummane, and Conn (2000) studied customer satisfaction among Australian human services call-center operations and reported that customer satisfaction was slightly higher in in-person services compared to call-center services. The observation supports the need for the current study of the determinants of customer satisfaction in help-desk services.

6. Barger and Grandey (2006), analyzing face-to-face service encounters (as different from online or on-telephone encounters), concluded that there was evidence to support that service with a smile resulted in higher perception of service quality and a higher level of customer satisfaction. Intensity of smile, pre-encounter smile, and postencounter smile were significant influencers of customer satisfaction.

7. Chen (2005) observed that many service encounters in the age of technology were in the nature of self-service technology encounters (SSTEs). SSTEs are technological interfaces where the customer produces service without the direct interpersonal involvement of a service employee; service over Internet is an example of SST. Chen concluded that the determinants of customer satisfaction in the SST and interpersonal encounters are different and suggested that critical incident technique or attribution technique be used to develop additional criteria for studying customer satisfaction in SST encounters.

8. Beatson, Lee, and Coote (2007) conducted exploratory qualitative analysis of service encounters in self-service technology sectors and suggested that quantitative studies should be undertaken. Söderlund and Julander (2003) studied the variable nature of services in encounters and its effect on customer satisfaction in the context of

trust and forgiveness. While other studies have concluded trust and customer satisfaction to be positively correlated (Garbarino and Johnson, 1999), results of the study by Söderlund and Julander suggested that forgiveness should not be taken for granted in cases where there is a poor service encounter, even if prior trust was established.

9. Aga and Safakli (2007) added firm image and price as additional variables in a modified SERVQUAL study and reported that there was support to suggest that both of these variables had significant impact on customer satisfaction. Aga and Safakali observed that firm image was the highest influencer of customer satisfaction, followed by price and service quality. The context of the study was the accounting services industry.

10. Hong and Goo (2004) also reported that customer satisfaction had a positive influence on a firm's image, and the reverse relationship may not be true.

11. Athanassopoulos and Iliakopoulos (2003) studied customer satisfaction in the telecommunications industry and identified two possible subsets of customer interactions: stable transactions and incident-based transactions. Incident based transactions (like fault repair in emergencies) had a greater effect on long-term overall customer satisfaction. Help-desk service encounters in the PC industry are incident-based transactions; study of customer satisfaction is, therefore, indicated.

12. Taking a different perspective, researchers have studied service-encounter failures and their effect on customer satisfaction. Michael (2004) studied service-encounter failures in financial service institutions and suggested adding a factor of perceived acceptability of failures as a possible measure of customer satisfaction.

13. Consumer dissatisfaction responses and complaint behavior were analyzed by Crie (2003) who proposed an integrated framework of the various theories of complaint behavior.

14. Boshoff and Staude (2003) also studied customer satisfaction from a failure-and-recovery perspective; investigating whether recovery effort after a service failure could return the customer to a state of customer satisfaction, the authors proposed an instrument RECOVSAT (satisfaction with service recovery).

15. Krampf, Ueltschy, and D'Amico (2003) investigated the role of emotion in service encounters and the effects emotion had on

customer satisfaction. Surprise, anger, delight, and shame were the emotional factors that were compared to disconfirmation factors. The study supported the hypothesis that while both emotion and disconfirmation influenced customer satisfaction positively, emotion had a greater influence.

16. Drawing upon theoretical foundations of ambivalence from the field of psychology and behavior, Olsen, Wilcox, and Olsson (2005) studied the effect of ambivalence (mixed emotions) on customer satisfaction and loyalty. The results suggested that ambivalent customers showed less satisfaction and less loyalty.

Service Quality and Customer Satisfaction

Service quality (SQ) has been linked to customer satisfaction by several researchers. While Bitner (1990) considered customer satisfaction as the antecedent of service quality, later research by Cronin and Taylor (1992) concluded that service quality was the antecedent of customer satisfaction. Studying quality in Web-portal services, Kuo et al. (2005) suggested that customer satisfaction was influenced by four service quality factors: empathy, ease of use, accessibility, and quality of information.

Zulganef (2006), in an empirical study of perceived service quality in the supermarket industry, concluded that overall customer satisfaction had a significant impact on customer relationship. Sharma and Ojha (2004) investigated service performance in the cell phone industry by using a psychometrically developed set of sixteen factors and arrived at a three-component measure for service performance as an antecedent to customer satisfaction. These three factors relate to service, network, and network operator performance. Froehle (2006) studied interaction of customer service representatives and technology like e-mail, telephone, and Internet chat in an effort to assess their impact on customer satisfaction; traditional factors like attentiveness, courtesy, and professionalism were found to have no significant effect on customer satisfaction in the technology context. Liu (2005) discussed the hierarchical nature and the multidimensionality of service quality. Liu summarized research points of view that indicated an organization's technical and functional quality, service environment, and service delivery in addition to some SERVQUAL dimensions while studying the service experience of customers.

Service Quality and Customer Satisfaction—The Cross-Cultural Context

Economidou-Kogetsidis (2005) studied telephone service encounters in a comparative study of Greek and English airline customers and observed that there were culture-influenced style differences ranging from interactional to transactional. Findings from the study suggested that telephone service encounters were influenced by sociocultural relativity with different degrees of perceived politeness, directness, courtesy, misunderstandings, and social distance. Perceived service quality of employees in the cross-cultural context was studied by Buda, Sengupta, and Elsayed-Elkhouly (2006). Culture-based differences in service quality were not observed in internal services received by the employees.

Laroche, Ueltschy, Abe, Cleveland, and Yannopoulos (2004) examined customer satisfaction in the context of cultural differences based on factorial experiments in the United States, Canada, and Japan. There were significant differences in the perceptions of service quality and failure forgiveness. Raghuram (2006) studied individual effectiveness at the service provider's end and concluded that differences in culture and context between the service providers and clients could have an adverse impact on customer service and client image.

A study of the intelligibility and comprehensibility of the English language conducted by Matsuura, Chiba, and Fujieda (MCF) (1999) concluded that even when the listeners felt the speech was easy to understand, the listeners could not correctly get the message and that listeners' perception of speech was influenced by several vocal factors. The MCF study compared American and Irish English in Japan. In outsourced help-desk services, US customers may encounter service providers from non-English-speaking countries. The findings of the MCF study indicated that there is merit in investigating some of the speech or communication-related variables for inclusion in the proposed study of customer satisfaction in help-desk services.

Measuring Customer Satisfaction

Some Empirical Models—Advantages and Shortcomings

Many models of customer satisfaction measurement are linked to the measurement of the antecedent service quality of the service encounter. One of the empirical models repeatedly seen in literature is the forty-four-item SERVQUAL approach developed by Parasuraman et al. (1988). Also referred to as the gap model, SERVQUAL defined perceived service quality gap as the difference between the expectation of service quality from the best provider and the perceived service quality from the current provider. The SERVQUAL uses five categories of service quality: (a) responsiveness, (b) reliability, (c) empathy, (d) tangible, and (e) assurance. These five categories were further divided into twenty-two variables that were measured.

Several authors (e.g., Buttle, 1996; Sureshchandar et al., 2001) have pointed out SERVQUAL's limitations. Cronin and Taylor (1992) pointed out deficiencies in SERVQUAL and suggested that the measurement of gap (and disconfirmation thereof) had no theoretical basis. An alternative approach based on the measurement of service performance (SERVPERF) with a twenty-one-item scale was suggested. Cronin and Taylor argued that the SERVPERF model takes better cognizance of the customer's attitudes, explains the variations in service quality better, and is a better predictor of purchase intentions. Van Dyke et al. (1997) voiced a concern that a single measure of service quality employed by SERVQUAL may not be suitable across industries; among the conceptual difficulties pointed out is the ambiguity of the expectations construct. Van Dyke et al. (1997) recommended the use of a measure other than the expectation gap score, especially in the information services sector. The SERVPERF scale has also been criticized as being too generic to indicate industry-specific dimensions of service quality (Cunningham, Young, and Lee, 2002). Saravanan and Rao (2007) suggested that SERVQUAL did not take into consideration the aspect of service marketing and that the content, convergent, and discriminant validity of SERVQUAL varied with the industry.

The original SERVQUAL was modified to include a measure called the zone of tolerance (ZOT). The ZOT is a tolerance band between the minimum adequate level and desired level of service (Parasuraman et al., 1988). Durvasula, Lobo, Lysonski, and Mehta (2006) used the ZOT approach to study two financial service industries in Singapore. Several authors have compared SERVQUAL and SERVPERF, but the conclusions vary from endorsements to criticism (Jain and Gupta, 2004; Johns, Avci, and Karatepe, 2004; Kettinger and Lee, 2005). Chaterjee and Chaterjee (2005) have tried the use of sixteen-parameter RIDIT (relative to an identified distribution) methodology from the biostatistics area.

A concept called service quality loss has also been used as another approach to measuring service quality. Taguchi and Clausing introduced the loss-function method in 1990 primarily for the manufacturing industry based on the concept that any variability in service introduced a cost, called the Taguchi loss. The Taguchi method has been criticized as being too restrictive as it is based on the single-response model (Liao, 2003). Later researchers have proposed modified loss-function approaches using multiresponse models (Chan and Ibrahim, 2004; Jeyapaul et al., 2005). Another quantitative approach, the PCR-TOPSIS (process capability ratio-theory of order preference by similarity to the ideal solution), was employed Liao (2003) to optimize multiresponse problems.

Drawing from the well-known Herzberg motivation-hygiene (M-H) theories, Kano (1974) proposed the M-H theory of quality considering five classes of quality based on satisfaction-dissatisfaction and functional-dysfunctional classification. Yang (2005) refined the Kano model by subdividing the classes further. Matzler et al. (2004) used the Kano approach coupled with regression analysis to study employee satisfaction. Kano's model has been combined with SERVQUAL by Chen and Lee (2006) to study dormitory service quality in a university setting. Using gap analysis similar to SERVQUAL, De Toni and Tonchia (2004) studied customer satisfaction in after-sales services, identifying eleven subjective and objective dimensions; eight gaps were analyzed.

Mukherjee and Nath (2005) compared the modified gap model, TOPSIS, and loss function models that are used to measure service quality. These models were derived from the theoretical areas of operational research and engineering. After studying customer satisfaction in the Indian banking industry, the authors concluded that while there was statistical agreement of customer-satisfaction rankings in the three methodologies, a single measure of the gap model could oversimplify the overall service quality measurement. The finding thus supports going away from gap-analysis approach.

Goode, Davies, Moutinho, and Jamal (2005) studied customer satisfaction in mobile phones using the multiple regression and neural network methods. With overall customer satisfaction as the dependent variable and eleven factors as independent variables, the authors concluded that the neural network method had higher robustness and reliability than the regression model and noted that the neural network approach had fewer assumptions and allowed for nonlinearity.

Jianan and DeSarbo (2005) studied the impact of customer heterogeneity on customer satisfaction. Based on the gap analysis model, the authors proposed a multidimensional scaling model to visualize attributes of customer satisfaction and customer differences. Burns, Graefe, and Absher (2003) compared the gap analysis to satisfaction-only scores in the recreation industry using multiple-regression analysis in an effort to assess which of the two was a better predictor of overall customer satisfaction. In the five service domains and nineteen attributes used in the study, the satisfaction-only measure was two to three times stronger. The finding supports the use of a multiple-regression approach in the current study of help-desk services in preference to gap analysis methodology.

Matzler, Sauerwein, and Heischmidt (2003) adopted an importance-performance analysis approach. The authors pointed out that basic factors, performance factors, and excitement factors are important service attributes. The study presented an analytical approach to identify these factors and suggested a way of extending the importance-performance analysis.

Roscino and Pollice (2004) measured customer satisfaction in automobile dealership using factor analysis. An important aspect of their methodology was the use of a polychoric matrix to impute and input ordinal and missing data into the factor analysis. The authors also used regression in analyzing the relationships among variables.

In a study of customer satisfaction in the sports-tourism industry in Europe, Beier, Woratschek, and Zieschang (2004) sought to remove some of the disadvantages of the SERVQUAL approach with the identification of service lacks (ISL) methodology. These disadvantages have been identified as the problems with definitions and measurement of expectation, importance, and adequacy. The ISL approach deals with aggregation of satisfaction factors using factor analysis and regression to test the relationships and ranking. In another study related to the recreation industry, Costa, Glinia, Goudas, and Panagiotis (2004) also moved away from SERVQUAL and suggested the measurement of animation experience as part of the sociopsychological input to customer satisfaction. The components of animation included (a) creativity, (b) social interaction, (c) discovery, (d) adventure, (e) action, and (f) return to self.

Kuo (2004) applied Kano's model to study service quality in the Web community using twenty-nine quality elements and suggested that diminishing customer dissatisfaction prevented further customer loss but did not create loyal or happy customers. McDevitt (2004) did a comparison of customer satisfaction in online and traditional customer interactions. Relationships between expectations, satisfaction, and repurchase intent were examined in the limited research study.

Kosciulek (2003) studied customer satisfaction in vocational rehabilitation services using a multidimensional scaling approach with fourteen stimuli. The results suggested, "Even with a relatively small number of stimuli, customer satisfaction studies could give stable and interpretable dimensions" (Kosciulek, p. 96). Kocakoç and Sen (2006) discussed the importance of surveys in customer-satisfaction studies. The authors suggested the use of an individual contribution to improvement score and a total contribution to improvement. The total contribution to improvement scores and factor analyses were used to pinpoint areas of improvement.

Effect of Measurement on Customer Behavior

Studying customer satisfaction may itself influence postsurvey behavior of the respondents. Morwitz (2005) investigated the impact of customer-satisfaction surveys using experimental and control groups. The study revealed that measuring satisfaction changed the behavior of the respondents in the experimental group. Quicker purchase, higher frequency of purchase, and positive attitudes toward the product were revealed in the experimental groups. These effects persisted over time.

Variables in This Research Study—Dependent Variable

The dependent variable in the research study was customer satisfaction. Based on various definitions of customer satisfaction found in literature (e.g., Bartikowski and Llosa, 2004; Garbarino and Johnson, 1999) and pursuant to the stated problem and purpose of the research study, the following working definition of customer satisfaction was arrived at in chapter 1 of the study: Customer satisfaction is a postservice evaluative judgment of a service encounter with a remote provider based on an assessment of the performance of various attributes that constitute that service.

Variables in this Research Study—Independent Variables

Literature reviewed so far indicated that there was a considerable overlap in the understanding of service quality and customer satisfaction. As stated earlier, service quality had been recognized as the antecedent of customer satisfaction. The determinants of service quality have been used, therefore, to measure customer satisfaction through SERVQUAL, SERVPERF, and other methodologies. For outsourced help-desk services delivered remotely, some of the variables (tangibles like clean facilities, neat appearance, etc.) used in other service quality studies were not applicable.

Background on Independent Variables

PC help-desk services by remote providers may have technology components of e-mail, telephone, and Internet chat accompanied by instructions that may be of a technical nature. Froehle (2006), in an exploratory study, examined the interaction of service providers and the technological interface and concluded, "Service representatives contributed to customer satisfaction more when they exhibited the characteristics of thoroughness, knowledgeableness, and preparedness, regardless of the richness of the medium used" (p. 5). While courtesy, attentiveness, and professionalism (normally applicable to face-to-face service encounters) did not significantly influence customer satisfaction in technology-related contexts, Froehle cautioned that these three variables should not be neglected in the study of customer satisfaction. It would be thus necessary to discuss the variable constructs that are broadly known to influence customer satisfaction, add variables that are specific to remote or outsourced providers, and arrive at a list of independent variables and their definitions for the study at hand. The literature review contains a study of the rationale for seven independent variable constructs: responsiveness, reliability, quality of communication, service attitude, empathy, quality of information, and ethics. The construct of each of these factors could be further explained by several component variables. The suitability of each factor and its components in the study are discussed in the following subsections.

Responsiveness

Responsiveness as an independent variable has been widely used in measuring service quality and the ensuing customer satisfaction. Introduced as a variable in the SERVQUAL instrument, *responsiveness* was defined as willingness in providing prompt service. Following SERVQUAL's popularity, other researchers have continued to use the definition of responsiveness in various studies of customer satisfaction in hospital, tourism, banking, and other industries. Kelley and Hurst (as cited in Piligrimienė and Bučiūnienė, 2008), focusing on the health care industry, defined responsiveness as the degree to which a service provider functions by placing the user at the center, or *customer centeredness*. Malhotra, Ulgado, Agarwal, Shainesh, and Wu (2005) studied quality of service in developed and developing countries and considered responsiveness as timely and substantive response to inquiries and complaints. In a study of online shopping (Bauer, Falk, and Hammerschmidt, 2006), responsiveness was considered to be made up of promptness of reaction, availability of personnel and alternative communication channels, and return policy on goods. Promptness and efficiency also appear as essential concepts in the constructs of responsiveness in a study of Internet banking (Liao and Cheung, 2008). Mattila and Mount (2006) investigated call-center responses in the hospitality industry and suggested that timeliness and problem resolution were important determinants of customer satisfaction. Based on the foregoing observations, *responsiveness* was defined in the current research study of PC help-desk services as a willingness to help, accompanied by courtesy, quick response, and a speedy resolution of the customer's concerns.

Reliability

Reliability was defined in SERVQUAL as "the ability to perform promised service dependably and accurately" (Parasuraman et al., 1988, p. 23). Bauer, Falk, and Hammerschmidt (2006) have expanded the reliability construct to include timeliness of service, range, availability of product or service, and confidentiality. In a study of customer satisfaction of Internet banking services in Hong Kong, Liao and Cheung (2008) suggested that error-free transactions, privacy, and security were measures of reliability. In the current study of PC help-desk services, *reliability* was defined in the study as a combination of five components: dependability, technical competence, availability on call, error-free instruction, and sincerity.

Quality of Communication

In the context of help-desk services provided over the telephone, verbal communication takes place following a call to the help desk. Boshoff and

Staude (2003), who studied service provider behaviors, discussed two types of communication styles: convergence and maintenance. *Convergence* occurs when the service provider's communication behavior (vocal, verbal, and nonverbal) and the customer's communication behavior become similar. *Maintenance style* does not seek the convergence. Boshoff and Staude's research specifically focused on customer satisfaction in a service-recovery situation; the authors concluded that satisfaction was primarily influenced by communication. Clarity of communication, the service provider's ability to understand the customer's issues, and a convergence style were indicated.

Although both help-desk service providers and customers are assumed to be able to understand English, clarity of spoken language may still be in question. In a study of intelligibility and comprehensibility of different spoken English in Japan, Matsuura, Chiba, and Fujieda (1999) tested the effects of accents, speed of delivery, intonation, fluency, grammar, vocabulary, vocal intensity, and pauses. Based on the study, Matsuura et al. suggested the following:

1. Listeners could not understand the purport of the message correctly even if the spoken utterance was clear.
2. The amount of exposure and familiarity to a particular variety of English could improve comprehensibility, not necessarily a better understanding of the message.
3. Familiarity with a specific variety of English could bring higher comprehensibility but might not increase the understanding of the message.
4. Clarity, intonation, fluency, and pauses affected the perception of speech.

Matsuura et al. (1999) recommended larger studies of different regional varieties of English to investigate the relationship between a particular regional variety and comprehensibility to the listener.

Considering the fact that PC help-desk services were being outsourced to non-native English-speaking countries (like India, the Philippines, China, and other countries), it was prudent and necessary to include quality of communication as a dependent variable in the current study. For the research study, *quality of communication* was defined as a construct based on a combination of fifteen concepts: acceptable speed of delivery of speech, accent, intonation, clarity of pronunciation, clarity of instruction, explanation, comprehensibility by customer, fluency in English, vocabulary, grammar, vocal intensity, pauses, ability to understand customer, live guidance through process, and follow-through.

Service Attitude

Behavioral aspects of service and their relation to customer satisfaction were studied in medical and restaurant services by Winsted (2000). Respect, attitude, genuineness, understanding, and demeanor were some of the measures used in Winsted's research that studied three groups of variables: concern, civility, and congeniality. Winsted concluded that these three groups of variables had significant impact on customer satisfaction and that there were similarities in their impact across the different industries studied.

For the research study of the help-desk services, an independent construct defined as service attitude was used incorporating the four components: concern for the customer, civility, congeniality, and genuineness in assisting the customer. Service attitude could be a predisposition of the service provider even before the customer discusses the service issue at hand, and continues during the service encounter.

Empathy

Parasuraman et al. (1988), while developing SERVQUAL, defined *empathy* as "caring, individualized attention provided to the customers" (p. 23). A closely related construct, assurance, was found not to have any distinction from empathy. In addition, while empathy did not have statistically significant regression coefficients, empathy was found to have a strong correlation to overall quality of service perceived by the customer (Parasuraman et al., 1988). Examining the influence of empathy, Aggarwal, Castleberry, Shepherd, and Ridnour (2005) surveyed 162 buyers and found that empathy had significant positive influence on listening, trust in the salesperson, and satisfaction. Kuo, Lu, Huang, and Wu (2005) studied customer satisfaction in Web-portal services and concluded that empathy had a significant influence on customer satisfaction.

Empathy, as an independent variable construct, was therefore included in the current study of PC help-desk services. *Empathy* was defined as expressed attitudes covering six aspects: expressions of caring remarks, consideration for the customer's time and urgency, listening patiently, trustworthiness, friendliness, and attentiveness.

Quality of Information

Quality of information was defined as a combination of four concepts: accuracy, timeliness, relevance, and the ease of use of information given to the customer (Kuo et al., 2005). Quality of information—encompassing provision of up-to-date, accurate, useful, and complete information—was studied as a variable in Web-quality satisfaction by Hsiu-Fen (2007) who concluded that quality of information had significant impact on customer satisfaction. PC help-desk services have a combination of technical and communication issues at both ends (Wegge, Vogt, and Wecking, 2007). Quality of information in PC help-desk services would therefore be included as an independent variable.

Ethics

Ethics in a service encounter combined the four expectations of security, privacy, nondeception, and a fulfillment of promise (Roman, 2007). Martinez-Tur, Peir, Ramos, and Moliner (2006) studied perceptions of justice as predictors of customer satisfaction. Distributive justice was found to be the most important predictor of customer satisfaction, followed by interactional and procedural justice. Questions seeking customers' inputs on perceived fairness of outcome (distributive component) and of personal treatment (interactional component) were therefore included in the survey questionnaire.

Gap in Literature

As noted in earlier sections, there are several customer-satisfaction studies in the hospital, banking, telecommunication, restaurant, sports, and leisure industries. The review of literature indicated that a study of customer satisfaction in help-desk services had the following complexities that were not normally present in a domestic service:

1. Technological services delivered by a remote global service provider
2. Virtual space and interaction across international time zones

3. Issues in communication arising out of cultural differences
4. Issues in communication arising out of language skills
5. Possible differences in the understanding of expectations by the service provider and receiver

Customer-satisfaction studies conducted in the last twenty years have not addressed the combination of the five areas of complexities listed above. Many of the studies were specific to a country and were focused on in-person services. Customer satisfaction in globally outsourced PC help-desk services had yet to be studied.

Implications to Business Leadership

The literature review presented so far has indicated that organizations need to make customer satisfaction a crucial objective. Linkage between customer satisfaction and firm success were discussed in the section. The leader's responsibility then would be to find avenues of enhancing customer satisfaction at various levels in the organization by monitoring every relationship with the customer.

- Payne and Frow (2005) developed a conceptual framework for CRM that helps broaden the understanding of CRM and its role in enhancing customer value and, as a result, shareholder value. Emphasizing the need for a cross-functional, process-oriented approach that positions CRM at a strategic level, the authors identified five key cross-functional CRM processes: a strategy development process, a value creation process, a multichannel integration process, an information management process, and a performance assessment process. Payne and Frow pointed out that customer satisfaction, a part of the value creation process and an important metric, reached only 36% of the board of directors.
- Discussing firm strategy, organizational alignment, and technology as part of CRM, Roberts, Liu, and Hazard (2005) considered customer satisfaction as one of three objectives—loyalty and retention being the other two.
- Ahearne, Mathieu, Rapp, and Adam (2005) studied customer satisfaction, employee empowerment, and the effect of leadership in the pharmaceutical industry. The results of the study suggested

that sales service employees with lower development benefit most from leader empowerment; the study also highlighted the importance of employee commitment to achieving customer satisfaction.

- Luo and Bhattacharya (2006) examined the linkages between corporate social responsibility, customer satisfaction, and market value creation. They determined that achieving customer satisfaction was one of the ways of realizing the financial returns and increasing the market value. Customer satisfaction accompanied by trust showed strong positive associations with customer retention and word-of-mouth promotion (Ranaweera and Prabhu, 2003).

- Cooil, Keiningham, Aksoy, and Hsu (2007) studied the relationship in customer-satisfaction levels to share of wallet in the Canadian banking industry and suggested that changes in customer satisfaction directly and nonlinearly influenced the share of wallet a customer apportions to a service or product. Managerial implication of the study for leaders was to strengthen strategies to improve and to reduce switching of customers to competitors.

- Lee and Hwan (2005) studied the relationship of customer satisfaction to corporate profitability in Taiwanese firms and concluded that customer satisfaction was indeed an antecedent to profitability.

- Ranaweera (2007), however, presented a different perspective in terms of long-term customer relationships, cautioning that long-term customers may not essentially be profitable.

- Smith and Wright (2004) studied customer satisfaction/loyalty in the PC industry and concluded that high customer loyalty resulted in a competitive advantage in the PC industry.

- The role of leadership in patient satisfaction in US hospitals was studied by Marley, Collier, and Goldstein (2004). The study supported the idea that patient satisfaction was, in fact, influenced by hospital leadership.

- Chandrashekaran, Rotte, Tax, and Grewal (2007) pointed out that the strength of customer satisfaction was also important, not merely the presence of satisfaction, in achieving long-term customer loyalty. Uncertainty and weak judgments of satisfaction in respect of a firm and its products or services increased customer vulnerability according to these authors.

Given the linkage between customer satisfaction, long-term survival, and profitability, the research study of globally outsourced help-desk services could assist leadership as follows:

1. The current study would likely bring out specific determinants of customer satisfaction in outsourced help-desk services. Not all factors used in the popular SERVQUAL or SERVPERF models might apply (Saravanan and Rao, 2007).
2. Grandey, Fisk, and Steiner (2005) observed that as firms outsource service functions, managers needed to take note of emotional strain on the employees and negative reactions from the local customers. The research study was expected to provide guidelines to leadership on training the service providers in addressing cultural and language barriers.
3. Leadership could address causes of dissatisfaction and achieve higher long-term customer retention and corporate profitability through a better understanding of customer satisfaction in the area. Leadership could target vulnerable customers to prevent defection to competitors (Chandrashekaran, Rotte, Tax, and Grewal, 2007; Lee and Hwan, 2005; Luo and Bhattacharya, 2006). Hence, the research study might help in improving the firm's image. Leadership needed to be aware that customer satisfaction has a positive impact on the firm's image (Aga and Safakli, 2007).

Customer satisfaction and CRM in the larger context were, therefore, important aspects of firm strategy that leaders of organizations have to pursue. Both customer satisfaction and CRM had shown specific and measurable impact on long-term profitability, shareholder value, competitive advantage, and value creation.

Conclusions

The literature review presented so far led to the following conclusions:

1. There was sufficient evidence to indicate that the issue of customer satisfaction was important from an organizational and societal perspective.

2. A transaction-specific customer-satisfaction measurement was better at understanding determinants of customer satisfaction and in guiding the leadership in improving customer satisfaction.

3. Customer satisfaction in outsourced PC help-desk services had not been studied, and there existed a gap in literature.

4. Popular methodologies like SERVQUAL were not best suited for the study, and other options were explored.

5. Seven independent variables (responsiveness, reliability, quality of communication, service attitude, empathy, quality of information, and ethics) were identified for the current study based on the stated problem, purpose, and the literature examined.

6. Heterogeneity at the consumers' end, firm reputation, and image would not be included as variables.

7. Customer satisfaction had been linked to firm strategy, revenue growth, and survival and was, therefore, significant to organizational leadership.

Chapter Summary

Globally outsourced services were on the increase, citing reasons of cost reduction and competitive advantage. However, there were concerns that such outsourcing may have negatively affected customer satisfaction. An assessment of the determinants of customer satisfaction in outsourced help-desk services was, therefore, likely to help managers in increasing customer satisfaction and in improving customer retention and long-term profitability.

A review of customer-satisfaction literature was undertaken to explore historical perspectives and current thinking. Definitions of customer satisfaction were explored, and a working definition for the study was suggested. Literature on service encounters and service quality were also examined. Cross-cultural effects in the context of global services were discussed. Various models and methodologies of measurement of customer satisfaction were discussed, and potential variables for the current study were identified. The literature review process concluded with an identification of the gap in literature and a discussion on implications to leadership.

The research study of customer satisfaction in perceived outsourced help-desk services had to consider variables that encompass responsiveness, reliability, communication, service behavior, empathy, ethics, and quality of information. The selection of the appropriate survey methodology and analytical tools will be discussed in the next chapter.

CHAPTER 3

RESEARCH METHODS

The purpose of the quantitative study is to identify the determinants of customer satisfaction and, in doing so, determine the relationship between several customer service factors and customer satisfaction of outsourced help-desk services in the PC industry. Customer satisfaction and its determinants have been studied extensively in the last twenty years in traditional industries including banking, health care, consumer goods, hospitality, and insurance. There are well-founded conceptual frameworks and extensive statistical methodologies for the study and analysis of customer satisfaction. Customer satisfaction with personal computer help-desk services remains unexplored.

The chapter contains a discussion on the rationale for the quantitative approach, the design appropriateness, and the rationale of how the methodology will achieve the goals of identification of the determinants of customer satisfaction and the determination of the relationship between several customer-service factors and customer satisfaction of outsourced help-desk services in the PC industry.

Research Method and Design Appropriateness

Customer satisfaction and its antecedents have been studied extensively in the last fifteen years, mostly in the traditional settings of the banking, insurance, travel, health care, and automotive industries. The meanings and purport of most independent variables are well-defined and understood, as elaborated in chapter 2. Exploratory qualitative methodology would, therefore, not be appropriate for the study. Quantitative approach is the chosen methodology for the proposed study of customer satisfaction in the PC help-desk industry. Research methodology and design appropriateness are discussed next.

Research Methodology

There are several empirical approaches that could be examined for the research study. These include direct observation of service, personal interview supported by a survey instrument, examining published quantitative data, mail or Internet surveys, and telephonic surveys. The study at hand involves identifying the determinants of customer satisfaction by assessing service attributes that the customers have experienced during a service encounter. Such an assessment by the customer is based on incident recall of a service encounter from the recent past. The survey methodology cannot thus be based on direct observation. Personal interviews with a questionnaire in hand and telephonic surveys are time-consuming and cost-prohibitive for the unsupported research study. Researcher fatigue would also be an issue when thousands of potential respondents are to be contacted. Internet—and e-mail-based surveys can reach thousands of potential respondents at a fraction of the cost.

Since customer services in the help-desk industry are generally not repetitive over time with a specific customer (as would be the case in automotive care, laundry, barbershops, groceries, and banks), a longitudinal study is not practical, nor is it considered necessary. The current research will be a cross-sectional study using data collected at a single point.

Rationale for Research Design and Analysis

As elaborated in the literature review in the previous chapter, research studies into customer satisfaction typically involve measuring customer attitudes and experiences through a survey. Two quantitative approaches have been used extensively in measuring customer satisfaction: gap analysis and performance analysis. The gap-analysis approach (seen in SERVQUAL and its modifications) aims to measure the difference between the expectation of service quality from the best provider and the perceived service quality from the current provider. Measurement and operationalization of perceived service quality as a gap depends on the customer having a set of well-formed expectations in the first place (see Buttle, 1996; Sureshchandar et al., 2001; van Dyke et al., 1997). In the case of PC help-desk services (unlike, for example, traditional and repeated services like laundry, hair salons, restaurants, and banks), technological aspects are involved; customers may not know what to expect.

Smith (1995), citing various studies, suggested that measurement of perceptions—rather than the gap—was equally effective and would probably avoid psychometric problems arising from the measurement of difference scores; midpoint responses and negative responses presented additional issues in the gap-analysis approach.

Gap-analysis approach, in the case of PC help-desk services, was therefore not the most appropriate method. Suuroja (2003) analyzed various studies on service quality (an antecedent of CS) that demonstrated that the quality of service should be assessed by a direct evaluation of service performance attributes and not as a gap from expectations. The present study used quantitative methodology and nonexperimental survey. The survey directly measured service performance attributes that formed components of the seven independent variable constructs.

Population and Sampling

Population for the study was all PC users based in the United States who sought help-desk assistance during 2008. The survey instrument was designed to elicit information from those who had a need to contact PC help-desk services. While the survey instrument sought to get PC ownership information specific to popular US makes of computers (like HP/Compaq, Dell, Apple, IBM, and Gateway), other foreign brands like Sony and Toshiba are also mentioned since customers may own one or more makes of computers or may have switched brands recently.

Sample Size

Since the number of PC owners is very large in the United States, sample size calculations were based on an unknown population number. Large samples do not necessarily produce results that are more accurate. Increases in sample sizes of small samples have a significant impact on reducing sampling errors, whereas proportional increases in large sample sizes have little impact on the degree of error (Neuman, 2003). A decision on sample size had to be based on degree of variability in the respondent population, accuracy requirements, number of variables studied, analysis requirements, and practical considerations of cost and time (Zodpey, 2004).

Sampling tables and nomograms are available for calculating sample sizes for various populations based on confidence levels and degree of sampling error. For a 95% confidence level and 5% sampling error, an adequate sample size is 385 for a population size of the order of up to 300 million (TRA, 2004). The sample size of 385 is also adequate from the point of view of statistical analysis involving multiple regression (Israel, 2003). A sample of four hundred usable responses was sought.

Informed Consent and Confidentiality

The study used an e-mail-based survey and was voluntarily answered. A preamble statement accompanying the survey instrument indicated the purpose of the survey and assured the respondents of the confidentiality of their responses (see appendix A). Informed consent was obtained through an informed consent paragraph followed by an *I Agree* button. Only the respondents who clicked on the *I Agree* button were able to proceed to the survey questionnaire. The respondents were not asked to indicate their name or any other identifiable personal information. The online consent data would be maintained on an external hard drive for a period of three years from the date of consent and destroyed thereafter.

Data Collection

The collection of data was done through the administration of a survey questionnaire to the sample described previously. McConkey, Stevens, and Loudon (2003) examined the effectiveness of service-sector surveys conducted using mail and Internet modalities. While Internet surveys produced a higher percentage of response rates, the difference in the response rates in the two modalities was not significant. McConkey et al. pointed out that Internet-based surveys delivered responses more quickly and with less cost, were easier for the respondents, and were able to reach geographically diverse populations easily; the authors concluded that an Internet survey was better than the medium of regular mail.

Data Collection Plan

In the current study of customer satisfaction in the PC help-desk service industry, the survey questionnaire was delivered through e-mail and Web link. The survey was sent to an opt-in e-mail database of PC and laptop computer users that had been procured for the survey. The survey instrument was prefixed with a paragraph explaining the authenticity of the researcher, the purpose of the survey, instructions on completing the survey, and indicated the time allowed for responses to be submitted. The responses were collected via a Web link in the e-mail where the survey resided.

The introductory paragraph to the survey in the e-mail briefly indicated the purpose of the survey, instructions for filling the survey, the deadline, and the researcher's authenticity, and embedded a Web link for the survey instrument. The e-mail was sent to an e-mail database of about two thousand potential respondents currently available with the researcher. The responses were received and stored in an electronic format for codification and further analysis. It was estimated that the survey questionnaire would take less than fifteen minutes to fill. At a conservative estimate, more than four hundred usable responses were anticipated. Respondents had ten days to respond. If there were fewer than four hundred usable responses, the survey was to be reissued to the nonrespondents and also to additional e-mail addresses. The data collected from the survey was stored by the researcher on an external hard drive not connected to the Internet. The data would be stored for three years from the closing date of the survey and would then be destroyed by the researcher. Nobody other than the researcher would have access to the survey data.

Instrumentation

The survey instrument was a questionnaire (see appendix A) containing questions designed to elicit responses related to demographic, independent, and intervening variables. The instrument used Likert-type items. Questionnaire construction took into account the types of questions, the number of Likert-scale points, intensity of language in the questions, length of the questionnaire, and the order of questions.

In the quantitative survey design, all items were closed-end questions. Anderson and Blackburn (2004) studied the effect of language intensity of e-mail surveys and concluded that there was evidence to suggest that higher levels of intense language provided significantly higher levels of response rates. Intensity of language referred to words and expressions that conveyed a sense of certainty, urgency, and command (as opposed to ambiguity, casualness, and request). With a larger response rate in mind, the questionnaire had been designed to include high-intensity expressions as much as possible.

Number of Scale Categories

Chang (1994) investigated the reliability and validity of using four-point and six-point Likert-type scales and concluded that criterion validity was not affected by the number of scale points. Chang recommended that the number of scale points should be decided on the empirical requirements of the specific study.

Preston and Coleman (2000) examined reliability, validity, discriminating power, and respondent preferences of various response categories ranging from two to eleven and observed that there was consistent support to the use of ten, nine, or seven response categories. The least preferred scales were those with two, three, or four response categories. Scales with five, seven, and ten responses were considered easy to use.

Owuor and Zumbo (2001) reported that for information accuracy, a four-point scale should be used at the minimum. However, Owuor and Zumbo also observed that fewer number of Likert-scale points resulted in increased bias; whereas, an increase in the number of points resulted in no substantial gain in information.

Coelho and Esteves (2007) studied the effects using five-point and ten-point scales in the context of the European Customer Satisfaction Index (ECSI). Nonresponse rates, response distribution, and validity issues were examined. Coelho and Esteves came to the conclusion that ten-point scale showed a higher convergent and discriminant validity. The ten-point scale also showed better explanatory power for the dependent variables—customer satisfaction and loyalty—in the ECSI. The same study showed that the five-point scale showed a higher attraction of responses to the midpoint.

Coelho and Esteves confirmed that there could be overestimation of response frequencies associated with the midpoint on a five-point scale.

Dawes (2007) examined whether data characteristics like measures of dispersion, shape, and central tendencies changed according to the number of Likert-type scale points. Dawes observed, in a split-sample study, that a five-point or seven-point scale was likely to produce higher mean scores compared to those produced by a ten-point scale. There were no significant differences in dispersion, skewness, or kurtosis. Dawes concluded that, from the point of getting information, these three scales were comparable for the use of confirmatory factor analysis.

Based on the previous discussions, the study on PC help-desk services used six-point Likert-type scale questions labeled only at anchor ends as shown in appendix A. Such a scale would have a higher reliability, lower respondent fatigue, a greater ability to ascertain directional responses, and would generate data that could be analyzed by parametric methodology.

In designing the questions, the seven independent variables and their forty-two components (outlined in chapter 1) were examined for synonymy, or close proximity of meanings, so that the number of questions could be reduced. Components that were synonymous were combined. For example, congeniality and friendliness were considered the same; genuineness and sincerity were treated as synonyms. The qualitative examination of variables resulted in reducing the total number of questions from forty-one to twenty-three (see appendix A). Table 3 shows the set of retained variables (questions 4 through 26) for the development of the survey instrument. These represent components of the seven independent variables.

Table 3
Retained Independent Variables and Their Components

Number	Question	Factors	Components
4	Service-provider was willing to help me.	Responsiveness	Willingness to help
5	Service-provider was courteous in his/her responses.	Responsiveness	Courtesy

6	My issues were resolved speedily.	Responsiveness	Quick response; Speedy resolution
7	Service-provider seemed to be technically competent.	Reliability	Technical competence

Table 3 *Continued*

Number	Question	Factors	Components
8	Service-provider was readily available when I contacted the service number.	Reliability	Availability on call
9	Service-provider spoke at a speed I could keep pace with.	Quality of communication	Acceptable speed of delivery of speech
10	Service-provider spoke with a heavy foreign accent.	Quality of communication	Accent
11	Service-provider's pronunciation was clear to me.	Quality of communication	Clarity of pronunciation; vocal intensity; pauses
12	The instructions given by the service-provider were clear.	Quality of communication	Clarity of instruction; explanation
13	Service-provider spoke in fluent English.	Quality of communication	Fluency in English
14	Service-provider seemed to be struggling to find the right words.	Quality of communication	Vocabulary
15	Service-provider understood my issues clearly.	Quality of communication	Ability to understand customer
16	I was guided by the service-provider as I continued to work on the issue.	Quality of communication	Live guidance through process
17	Service-provider followed-up to ensure my issue was resolved.	Quality of communication	Follow-through.

| 18 | Service-provider had a friendly attitude. | Service attitude | Congeniality |

Table 3 *Continued*

Number	Question	Factors	Components
19	Service-provider was not sincere in his/her efforts to help me.	Service attitude	Genuineness
20	I felt cheated by the service-provider.	Ethics	Nondeception
21	Service-provider understood my urgency.	Empathy	Consideration
22	He/she listened to me patiently	Empathy	Listening patiently
23	I could trust the service-provider to solve my issue.	Empathy	Trustworthiness
24	The information given to me was relevant in resolving my issue.	Quality of information	Relevance; accuracy
25	I could trust the service-provider to safeguard my personal information	Ethics	Security expectations
26	Service-provider was caring.	Service attitude	Concern

As a means of maintaining respondent focus and attention, three questions (19, 26, and 27) had been reversed. Nicholls, Orr, Okubo, and Loftus (2006) suggested that inclusion of reversed items may reduce the effect of pseudoneglect (an attentional bias favoring left-sided stimuli). While the practice of including reversed items is common in Likert-type surveys, response to reversed items may also introduce other sources of error.

Three types of misresponses associated with reversed items have been identified: acquiescence, inattention, and item verification difficulty. Methodologies are available for identifying and analytically adjusting such misresponses in reversed items; and these would be explored, if necessary, during the analysis phase of the survey data (Swain, Weathers, and Niedrich, 2008).

Instrument Reliability and Validity

Reliability is the extent to which repeated measurements with the survey instrument yield the same results. Reliability is, therefore, the degree to which observations or measures are free from variance arising out of random error. When high reliability exists, the survey questionnaire should reflect a true measure of customer satisfaction. While there are several ways of measuring reliability, Cronbach's alpha has been extensively used in several customer-satisfaction studies and will also be used in the study. Cronbach's alpha is calculated using covariance matrix of items in the survey instrument.

In determining acceptable reliability levels for Cronbach's alpha, George and Mallory (2003) categorize coefficients higher than 0.9 as excellent, higher than 0.8 as good, and higher than 0.7 as acceptable. Cronbach's alpha lower than 0.7 would be unacceptable. The study aimed to achieve a Cronbach's alpha of 0.80.

Pilot Study for Determining Reliability

For the purpose of establishing instrument reliability through Cronbach's alpha, the survey instrument was administered to twenty randomly selected respondents in a pilot study. Administration was by way of e-mail/Internet, and the pilot study provided information on the appropriateness of the data-collection approach. Using a statistical package (e.g., SPSS or Minitab), the following were calculated in the pilot study (Gliem and Gliem, 2003):

1. Summated scores for the scale

2. Summary means and variances
3. Inter-item correlations
4. Calculation of means, variances, and correlations by deleting individual items
5. Cronbach's alpha after item is removed
6. Final Cronbach's alpha coefficient of internal consistency

The final Cronbach's alpha should be 0.80 or higher after iterations of deleting certain items. Internal consistency would be achieved by rewording, reordering, and retesting. After having achieved internal consistency, the instrument would be tested for internal and external validity.

Instrument Validity

Instrument validity has three components: criterion-related validity, content validity, and construct validity. These three aspects are addressed here in respect of the research design and instrument in the current study.

Criterion-Related Validity

Criterion-related validity (CRV) indicates how closely the criteria (the seven independent variables with their components) in the survey questionnaire measure an external behavior (the dependent variable—customer satisfaction, in this case) based on other well-established criteria. The detailed discussion about each variable presented in chapter 1 and the extensive literature review in chapter 2 established that the seven independent variables were valid candidates to measure customer satisfaction. CRV can be effectively ascertained in experiments where the outcomes can be measured in numbers or test scores (as in IQ tests or SAT scores); measurement of CRV may not be applicable to all situations and studies, especially while researching abstract concepts (for example, customer satisfaction).

Content Validity

Content validity (CV) represents the extent to which the criteria measured through the survey questionnaire represent the domain of customer satisfaction. Content validity is also called face validity. As in criterion-related validity, content validity is difficult to ascertain when the dependent variable is abstract in nature, like customer satisfaction. In the current study of customer satisfaction, content validity was performed on the survey instrument using a panel of academicians and typical respondents. The *interrater agreement (IRA)* was used to determine content validity. A content validity of 80% would be the acceptable threshold to use the instrument without further revisions (i.e., at least 80% of the questions should be considered by the panel as representing the concept to be measured; Rubio, Berg-Weger, Tebb, Lee, and Rauch, 2003).

Construct Validity

Construct validity indicates the extent to which a measure performs with respect to theoretically derived expectations. Construct validity in the current study was assessed by factor analysis using a statistical package.

Validity—Internal

Validity depends on the extent of nonrandom error in a set of observations. Internal validity aims "to eliminate alternative explanations of the dependent variable" (Neuman, 2003, p. 251). Threats to survey validity may come from researcher-based factors, subject-based factors, or external factors as enumerated in Neuman (2003). The nine types of threats to internal validity identified by Neuman are discussed in the following section with reference to the study at hand.

Threats and Remedies to Internal Validity

1. History: History effects relate to external influences that affect the dependent variables when respondents are measured over time or repeatedly. The current study of PC help-desk services was a

cross-sectional study; the survey instrument took less than fifteen minutes to complete. The respondent was measured only once, and thus, threats arising from history effects did not exist.

2. Maturation: This refers to learning experiences or attitudinal changes during the survey because of lapse of time and episodes of learning. The current study of PC help-desk services was a cross-sectional study, and the survey itself was estimated to take less than fifteen minutes. The impact of maturation did, therefore, not pose a threat.

3. Testing: When a dependent variable is measured at two different times and an independent variable is introduced in the interim, a threat to survey could ensue. Such a threat was eliminated in the current study as there were no longitudinal measurements and no independent variable was introduced during the course of the study.

4. Instrumentation: Threat of instrumentation arises when the means of measuring the dependent variable changes during the course of the study. In the current study, an identical survey instrument will be sent via e-mail/Internet to all potential respondents, and no changes will be made to the instrument during the survey. There were no mechanical or human observations also. Thus, the threat arising out of instrumentation was eliminated.

5. Regression: During repeated longitudinal measurements of the dependent variable, extreme values could tend toward the mean value in a statistical regression effect. Such regression threat was not present in the current study as there were no repeated or longitudinal measurements over time.

6. Selection: The threat of selection bias occurs when one of the surveyed or experimental groups has a characteristic that affects the results beyond randomness. The current study of help-desk services was a cross-sectional study of one random group from an e-mail address database of unknown demographics and traits, and thus was not susceptible to selection bias.

7. Experimental mortality: Mortality represents loss of respondents during the course of an experiment. In addition to death, loss of respondents could occur in a longitudinal experiment because of sickness, survey fatigue, and geographical displacement. As stated in (2) above, the current study of PC help-desk services was a

cross-sectional study, and the survey itself took less than fifteen minutes.

8. Selection maturation-interaction: If the selected sample groups are studied over time, the natural maturation process may interfere with a true measurement of the dependent variable with respect to the independent variables with which the study was originally conceived. The threat of selection-maturation would be absent in the current study since there was no time-lapse. The current study was cross-sectional in nature.

9. Researcher bias: Researcher bias occurs when potential respondents are in some way influenced by the researcher who may be expecting a specific outcome. The bias was eliminated in the current study by the researcher not having any prior contact with any of the potential respondents. The only subjects that would have seen the questionnaire would be the pilot study group, and that group was excluded from the main e-mail survey.

There were no groups to be selected. Testing bias could occur when, during the course of the experiment, an event happened that affected the premise or the outcome. Testing bias of this nature would be specific to longitudinal experiments and, therefore, was effectively eliminated in the cross-sectional study.

Validity—External

External validity is the generalizability of the findings of the study to events and circumstances external to the specific research (Neuman, 2003). The questions in the survey covered concepts and constructs that were common to help-desk services in other business sectors like banking, health, insurance, and telecommunication. Except for one demographical question about the make of the PC owned, all questions had been designed to be generalizable. There were no specific restrictions on the sample or the population. The instrument had no surprise or novelty and was realistic. The findings of the study would therefore be generalizable and would meet external validity.

Approaches to Data Analysis

As explained in chapter 1, parametric techniques were used for the analysis of Likert-type data collected in the study. Previous discussion of seven groups of independent variables and more than thirty component parts pointed toward a multivariate statistical analysis that could ultimately reduce the number of variables and yet better explain customer satisfaction in the current study. Further, the multivariate analyses would help generate useful hypotheses that could be statistically tested. Since the purpose of the research was to identify the determinants of customer satisfaction in PC help-desk services and to assess their degree and direction of influence, the statistical techniques chosen for the study are factor analysis, multivariate regression, and two-tailed hypothesis testing at 95% confidence level.

Data collected by the survey were to be coded, checked, corrected for missing data, and analyzed using factor analysis and multiple regression analysis. Factor analysis could reduce the number of components that explained the relationship between the variables. Regression analysis would then assess the degree and direction of relationship among the variables.

Treatment of Missing Data

Several well-developed methods are available for the treatment of missing data. A simple approach for handling missing data is to exclude the entire response from the analysis. This would obviously reduce the number of usable responses and, in some cases, might introduce biased estimates. Other options involve weighting of included responses to compensate for excluded responses, regression-based imputation, single and multiple imputations, and maximum-likelihood imputation based on incomplete data. These options have been discussed by several researchers (e.g., Fox-Wasylyshyn and El-Masri, 2005; O'Rourke, 2003; Raghunathan, 2004; Saunders et al., 2006). While detailed explanations of these statistical methods are beyond the scope of the chapter, it was proposed to use a mean-substitution method to impute a missing data point. The use of such imputation by the mean would be restricted, and if in a response more than 15% of data points are missing, the response would be excluded (Fox-Wasylyshyn and El-Masri, 2005).

Chapter Summary

Reiterating the purpose of the study, research methodology and appropriateness of design were discussed in the chapter. Issues concerning the choice of method, choice of scale points, and choice of the analytical methods were discussed and academically supported arguments were presented, leading to the selection of an ends-only-labeled Likert-type six-point scale as the appropriate scale. Based on this, a survey instrument was designed to elicit responses in respect of independent, intervening, and dependent variables. Approaches for assessing reliability and validity were indicated. Threats to survey validity were explained and remedies indicated. The survey instrument was administered through Internet and e-mail platforms, seeking a minimum of four hundred responses. Analysis would be made using parametric methodology of factor analysis and multiple regression. A procedure for the treatment of missing data was indicated. The following chapters contain presentations of study findings and conclusions flowing logically from those findings.

CHAPTER 4

DATA COLLECTION AND ANALYSES

Based on the methodology explained in chapter 3, data collection and analyses were undertaken within the US population, aiming at getting at least four hundred usable responses and employing the following processes:

1. A review of the survey instrument (appendix A) by using feedback from scholars and peers. The aim was to achieve an interrater agreement of at least 80% as suggested by Rubio, Berg-Weger, Tebb, Lee, and Rauch (2003).
2. Refining of survey-instrument language based on the above feedback.
3. Pilot test of the survey instrument with survey of thirty potential respondents.
4. Remedy of any technical problems in the administration of e-mail survey.
5. Launching the e-mail survey.
6. Data collection and conversion to SPSS-compatible format.
7. Dealing with missing data.
8. Analyses and interpretation.

Interrater Agreement and Instrument Refinement

Survey instrument with additional review columns (appendix B) was sent to a pool of ten random reviewers comprising doctoral faculty and graduate faculty members. The purpose of the review was to detect any ambiguity of words or expressions and to assess whether the Likert-type questions used in the instrument were a reasonable representation of the measures of underlying factors. Seven responses were returned with suggestions and remarks. An 87% rating was obtained on clarity and a 95% rating was obtained on the questions being representatives of what they sought to measure. A level of 80% interrater agreement (IRA) is considered the minimum for a good survey questionnaire (Rubio, Berg-Weger, Tebb, Lee, and Rauch, 2003). A summary of responses is given in table 4.

Table 4
Interrater Agreement Summary

	Interrater agreement	
Response	Clarity	Conceptual agreement
	Yes	Yes
1	92%	100%
2	92%	100%
3	80%	NA
4	80%	100%
5	86%	85%
6	90%	93%
7	88%	92%
Average	87%	95%

Refining Final Survey Instrument

The reviewers gave suggestions for improving the readability of the instrument by changing certain words or phrases. All the suggestions were carefully considered and changes in wordings and phrases were made as shown in appendix C. No questions were added or deleted.

The final survey instrument and the accompanying e-mail are shown in appendix D. The e-mail introducing the survey contained information about the academic purpose of the survey, preservation of confidentiality of the respondents, and the destruction of survey data after three years. The first question on the survey instrument pertained to informed consent. The question was designed with a skip-logic that allowed only those who clicked on the *AGREE* button (indicating informed consent) to participate in the survey. Those who opted to click on *DISAGREE* were directly taken to the *Thank-You* note at the end of the survey.

Pilot Test

A pilot e-mail was sent to thirty respondents. The twenty-eight-question survey took less than two and a half minutes to complete on average. The target population of thirty e-mail addresses for the pilot test was chosen randomly from a database of potential respondents among PC/laptop buyers within the United States.

Data collected from the pilot survey showed the following:

1. There seemed to be no ambiguity in understanding the questions or the scale.
2. There were differences in the respondents' scoring of various questions on the Likert-type questions, indicating that the customer experiences were different.
3. There was also a difference in the level of customer satisfaction, the dependent variable.
4. The answers seemed to convey that the respondents might not have had difficulty in recalling their service encounters with the help-desk services.

The previous observations were indicative that further changes in the instrument were not needed and that the technological aspects of fielding the survey were adequate. The main survey could be launched.

Main Survey

The main survey was launched to a pool of potential respondents from a commercially obtained database of computer buyers in the previous one year. The database was procured from what is known as an *opt-in* list where the potential respondents have indicated their willingness to receive e-mail surveys. The survey was scheduled to be kept open for about fourteen days or until four hundred completed responses were received. Excluding the pilot test, 1,263 e-mails were sent out; 298 respondents opted out or turned in incomplete responses. No response was received from 499 persons. In all, 466 responses were returned complete without missing data, and these have been retained for analysis. This makes a 36.90% response rate. The data from the responses were collated in SPSS-compatible format for further analyses.

Analyses of Data and Findings

In analyzing the data collected from the Likert-type survey instrument, parametric analysis has been used as explained in chapter 1. An assumption of interval-type data has been made since the survey instrument had descriptive anchors only at the ends and no descriptors among the intermediate points of the six-point scale. Tendency to mark off the central point was expected to be reduced by the use of an even-numbered scale. The analyses of collected data proceeded in ten steps as follows:

1. Codification of SPSS data
2. Checking of missing data and remedies thereof
3. Reverse coding of three questions that were intentionally context-reversed
4. Demographic analysis
5. Diagnosis and reduction of multicollinearity
6. Checking of internal reliability
7. Comparison of means and variances

8. Check for sampling adequacy for factor analysis
9. Reduction of variables through factor analysis
10. Univariate multiple regression

These steps are explained in following sections.

Codification of SPSS Data

The data from the survey were recorded in SPSS-compatible format and coded under variables Q3 through Q30 as shown in appendix E. These code designations will be used, hereafter, while referring to the questions on the survey instrument. Code Q1 was the variable identification row per SPSS format requirements. Code Q2 was used for the informed consent skip-logic question and, thus, does not appear in the data set. The collected data had an array of 466 rows and 28 columns.

Missing Values

SPSS check confirmed that that there were no missing values in these 466 cases. The usable sample size thus met the minimum requirement of four hundred responses consistent with the research design for the study. There was no need to impute any data points.

Reverse Coding

The following three questions with negative connotations were intentionally reversed on the survey instrument to keep respondent attention.

1. Q16: Service-provider seemed to be struggling to find the right words.
2. Q21: Service-provider was not sincere in his/her efforts to help me.
3. Q22: I felt cheated by the service-provider.

The collected data for these three questions were reverse coded in order to give the correct directional interpretation on the *Strongly Disagree* to *Strongly Agree* scale.

Demographic Analysis

An examination of the demographic data collected in the survey showed that out of the 466 respondents, 197 were male and 269 female. The survey was not designed to study customer (respondent) heterogenity as a factor in assessing the determinants of customer satisfaction in help-desk services. General observations linking the demographics to the dependent variable have been made in later sections.

As part of the demographic data, the survey instrument asked the respondents to identify the brand of PC/laptop about which they had called the help-desk. The data are summarized in figure 3.

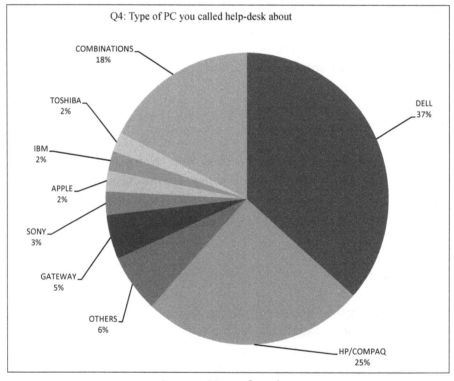

Figure 3. Type of product

The survey focused on a database of recent buyers (less than one year ago at the time of study) of PC/laptop computers in order to assure a reasonably accurate incident recall. Out of the 466 respondents, 174 (37.3%) had contacted the help-desk services less than three months prior to the survey.

Important to the study was the source of help-desk services. As explained in chapter 1, the survey had limitations in that the survey could only gather the perceived source as indicated by the respondents. In reality, it is the respondent who makes the judgment, based on the service encounter, whether he or she was serviced by someone based overseas and to what extent such encounter resulted in the customer's satisfaction. Thus, perceived source is relevant. Based on data collected for question Q30, 264 (57%) respondents perceived that the source of their help-desk services was in the United States, whereas 202 (43%) thought the source was in a foreign country.

Diagnosis and Reduction of Multicollinearity

Multicollinearity occurs when two or more independent variables are highly correlated. Although the predictability of the dependent variable is not affected, multicollinearity of independent variables affects the measurement of the nature and degree of the effect of each independent variable. One way of reducing multicollinearity is to remove highly correlated independent variables in the survey instrument if they qualitatively measure similar variables. Field (2005) suggests a minimum acceptable value of determinant to be 0.00001 to avoid problems of multicollinearity.

Internal correlation was run among independent variables (Q4 to Q28). Multicollinearity (with all independent variable questions present) was measured by the value of determinant as 5.666E-09, which was unacceptably low. Based on the values of correlation coefficients, six questions—Q14, Q15, Q20, Q25, Q26, and Q28—were identified as possible candidates for removal. The arguments in favor of their removal are as follows:

Q14: The Instructions Given by the Service-Provider Were Clear.

The question, representing the construct *quality of communication,* has a relatively high correlation of 0.705 with Q11 (Service-provider spoke at a speed I could understand) and 0.804 with Q13 (Service-provider pronunciation was clear to me). While Q14 would give an indication of clarity, retaining Q11 and Q13 would give more information than Q14 alone in explaining clarity in terms of speed and pronunciation. Q14 was therefore deleted from further consideration.

Q15: Service-Provider Spoke in Fluent English.

Also representing *quality of communication*, Q15 had a correlation of 0.790 with Q13 (Service-provider pronunciation was clear to me). Moderately high correlation was seen with respect to Q11 (0.639) and Q14 (0.699). Negative moderate correlation

(-0.614) existed with Q12 (Service-provider spoke with a heavy foreign accent). Q11, Q12, and Q13 could be used to explain clarity and fluency in terms of speed, pronunciation, and accent, thereby, providing more information for managerial action where needed. Q15 was therefore dropped from further analyses. Q11, Q12, and Q13 were retained.

Q20: Service-Provider Had a Friendly Attitude.

Q20 pertains to the concept *service attitude*. Q20 would seem to be important as an independent variable in assessing customer satisfaction. However, within the framework of the survey instrument, one could explore other variables that could possibly deconstruct *friendly attitude* into practical and actionable components. An examination Q20 revealed a higher correlation (0.734) with Q24 (Service-provider listened to me patiently) than with other variables. Moderate correlation of 0.649 was seen with Q6 (PC/laptop service-provider was willing to help me) and of 0.680 with Q7 (Service-provider was courteous while providing responses). Q6 (courtesy) and Q7 (willingness to help) seem to be better explanatory concepts of *friendly attitude*. Q20 was therefore not considered for inclusion. Q6 and Q7 were retained.

Q25: I Could Trust the Service-Provider to Solve My Issue.

Q26: The Information Given to Me Was Relevant in Resolving My Issue.

These two questions are covered under the concepts of *empathy* and *quality of information* relating to trust and resolution of the issue. Q25 was highly correlated with four questions: Q8 (My issues were resolved speedily), with a correlation coefficient of 0.725; Q9 (Service-provider seemed to be technically competent), with a correlation coefficient of 0.737; Q17 (Service-provider understood my issues clearly), with a correlation coefficient of 0.778; and Q23 (Service-provider understood my urgency), with a correlation coefficient of 0.717. Q26 was well correlated with Q9 (Service-provider seemed to be technically competent), with a correlation coefficient of 0.719, and Q17 (Service-provider understood my issues clearly), with a correlation coefficient of 0.713. Moderate to high correlation was found with Q8 (My issues were resolved speedily), Q18 (I was guided by the service-provider as I acted on his/her instructions), and Q24 (Service-provider listened to me patiently). Both Q25 and Q26 were not considered further as other related questions seemed to provide better depth in further analyses.

Q28: The Service-Provider Was Caring.

The question was initially covered under the concept of *ethics* in the schema presented in chapter 1 (figure 2). Q28 was found to have correlations ranging from 0.735 to 0.604 in respect of questions Q6, Q7, Q8, Q9, Q17, Q18, and Q23 through Q27. Response to all these questions provide more information than Q28 about the caring aspect (for example, willingness, courtesy, speedy resolution, understanding of issue, and trust). Q28 was, therefore, chosen to be dropped from further consideration.

After the removal of these six questions, the survey had seventeen independent variables for analyses instead of twenty-three. Determinant of the reduced set of variables increased to 1.603E-05 (i.e., 0.00001603), thus satisfying the minimum requirement of 0.00001 for non-multicollinearity.

Internal Reliability

Internal reliability analysis of the seventeen independent variables was conducted using Cronbach's alpha method. Results are shown in table 5.

Table 5
Internal Reliability Test—Cronbach's Alpha

	Mean	Minimum	Maximum	Range
Item means	4.36	2.871	4.974	2.103
Item variance		1.732	0.2541	
Inter-item correlations	0.370	-0.596	0.766	1.362

Inter-item variance		1.285	0.838
Cronbach's alpha	0.889		
Standardized alpha	0.909		

Traditional research has used Cronbach's alpha level of 0.7000 for an acceptable reliability and 0.8000 for good reliability. The survey instrument used in the study has exceeded these requirements of internal validity.

Comparison of Means and Variances

Appendix F shows the means of the seventeen independent variables in descending order for all 466 observations. Items marked with an asterisk (*) were originally reversed in context on the survey instrument and needed to be interpreted in the opposite sense. On a six-point scale of *Strongly Disagree* to *Strongly Agree*, fifteen variables show a rating of 4.0 or higher. Courtesy, willingness to help, sincerity, patient listening, technical competence, and live guidance scored high on the survey ratings. Q12 (Service-provider spoke with a heavy foreign accent) received a score of 3.745, indicating that respondents were tending to disagree that they were spoken to with a heavy foreign accent. The lowest score of 2.871 was received by Q19 (Service-provider followed-up a few days later to ensure my issue was resolved), which indicates an area for improvement in terms of after-service follow-up.

Comparison of Grouped Means by Perceived Source of Help-Desk Services

Given the fact that there have been concerns reported regarding the quality of outsourced services (Marshall and Heffes, 2005; Scott, 2007), survey data were separated into two sets—one set where the respondents had perceived the service provider as from USA (US provider) and the other set where the respondents had perceived the service provider as being from a foreign country (foreign provider)—based on Q30. The grouped means are shown in appendix G.

Means for these two sets of seventeen questions were compared using two-tailed t-tests at a significance level of 0.05. Results are reported in appendix L. The difference in means was found to be significant in every one of the seventeen questions. In all but one question (Q12: Service-provider spoke with a heavy foreign accent), the US provider received more favorable ratings than the foreign provider did. This would suggest that respondents rated their experiences from perceived US help-desk services more positively than those from perceived foreign outsourced services did.

Gender: Comparison of Grouped Means

Means and variances in these two gender groups were compared using two-tailed t-tests at 95% confidence level. Results (table 6) suggested that there was no significant difference between genders in the perception of overall satisfaction.

Table 6
Gender and Satisfaction

	Gender	N	Mean	Std. deviation	Std. error mean
Overall, I was satisfied with help I received from service provider.	Male	197	4.381	1.516	0.108
	Female	269	4.353	1.627	0.099
	t = 0.186		df = 464		p = 0.853

Dependent Variable: Comparison of Grouped Means

The mean of the dependent variable (Q29: Overall, I was satisfied with help I received from service-provider) was compared for the US and foreign sources. The mean overall satisfaction was not only lower with perceived foreign-service providers, but also had higher standard deviation as seen in table 7. Higher standard deviation in satisfaction could suggest lax quality and consistency at the perceived foreign-provider end, other factors being equal. T-test at 0.05 significance level showed that the inequality was statistically significant (p<0.001), suggesting that there was indeed a lower level of satisfaction when the help-desk services were non-US based (table 8).

Table 7
Dependent Variable: Comparison of Grouped Means

	Perceived source	N	Mean	Std. deviation	Std. error mean
Overall, I was satisfied with help I received from service provider	U.S.A.	264	4.852	1.253	0.077
	A foreign country	202	3.728	1.731	0.122

Table 8
Dependent Variable: Test for Equality of Grouped Means

	Levene's test for equality of variances		t-test for equality of means					
	F	Sig.	t	df	Sig. (2-tailed)	Std. error difference	95% Confidence interval of the difference	
							Lower	Upper
Equal variances assumed	56.0798	4.5E-13	8.133	464.000	p<0.001	0.138	0.853	1.396
Equal variances not assumed			7.801	351.468	p<0.001	0.144	0.841	1.408

Sampling Adequacy for Factor Analysis

Kaiser-Meyer-Olkin (KMO) method measures partial correlations and is used for determining sampling adequacy for conducting factor analysis. The recommended minimum value for KMO measure is 0.50 (Pett, Lackey, and Sullivan, 2003). Survey data for 446 responses produced an acceptable KMO of 0.926, which is considered "marvelous" by Kaiser (cited in Pett et al., p.78), assuring sampling adequacy for factor analysis. Bartlett's sphericity test checks the null hypothesis that the correlation matrix is an identity matrix. An identity matrix (with main diagonal having values of one, and all nondiagonals being zeros and, hence, no correlations among variables) would not allow factor analysis to be used effectively. Variables need to be correlated in order to carry out factor analysis. Bartlett's test of sphericity on SPSS showed the significance level to be lower than 0.001, indicating that there was evidence to conclude that the correlation matrix was not an identity matrix. Table 9 has summarized these findings.

Table 9
KMO and Bartlett's Tests

Kaiser-Meyer-Olkin measure of sampling adequacy		0.926
Bartlett's test of sphericity	Approx. chi-square	5062.376
	df	136
	Sig.	$p < 0.001$

Reduction of Variables through Factor Analysis

Factor analysis allows the grouping of independent variables into classes that could present common themes among a set of independent variables and, thereby, reducing the number of variables for regression analysis. Factor analysis provides a basis for redefining constructs from the underlying concept variables. From a qualitative perspective, the extracted factors need to have a meaningful construct of variables and should be capable of explaining at least 80% of the variance. Several iterations of factor analysis using principal components analysis (PCA) were carried out on the seventeen independent variables using the following variations:

1. Run A: The entire data set of seventeen independent variables seeking Eigenvalues higher than 1.00.
2. Run B: The entire data set seventeen independent variables seeking seven factors.
3. Additional runs with four, five, and six factors.

In each case, Varimax rotation was used. Appendices H, I, and J show the detailed outputs of runs A and B. The results are summarized in table 10.

Table 10
Summary of Factor Analysis on Seventeen Independent Variables

	Data set used based on Q30	Criterion	Extracted factors	Variance explained
Run A	Both U.S. and foreign	Eigenvalues > 1.0	Three	66.08%
Run B	Both U.S. and foreign	Seven factors	Seven	81.80%

Several other PCA runs for four, five, and six factors showed explained variance percentages of 67.36, 74.98, and 78.50, respectively. These were not considered for further analyses.

Tables 11 and 12 show rotated component matrices for run A and run B respectively. Highlighted items show factor loadings higher than 0.600 in tables 11 and 12. One exception in table 12 is the statement: *Service provider spoke at a speed I could understand,* which has the value of 0.477 as its highest loading. Because nearly 82% variance could be explained by seven factors, only results of run B were retained for further consideration.

Table 11
Run A: Factor Analysis Seeking Eigenvalues >1.00

Independent variable	Component		
	1	2	3
My issues were resolved speedily.	0.790		
Service-provider seemed to be technically competent.	0.738	0.348	
Service-provider understood my issues clearly.	0.696		0.376
Service-provider was readily available when I contacted the service number.	0.692		
Service-provider understood my urgency.	0.679		
I could trust the service-provider to safeguard my personal information.	0.658		
Service-provider spoke at a speed I could understand.	0.654		0.443
Service-provider listened to me patiently.	0.596	0.529	
Service-provider followed-up a few days later to ensure my issue was resolved.	0.592		
I was guided by the service-provider as I acted on his/her instructions.	0.547	0.543	
Service-provider was NOT sincere in his/her efforts to help me.*		0.821	
I felt cheated by the service-provider.*		0.718	0.367
PC/laptop service-provider was willing to help me.	0.591	0.625	
Service-provider was courteous while providing responses.	0.589	0.599	
Service-provider spoke with a heavy foreign accent.*			-0.875
Service-provider seemed to be struggling to find the right words.		0.433	0.718
Service-provider pronunciation was clear to me.	0.592		0.624

* Reversed context

The seven factors obtained in run B seem to suggest a regrouping of the seventeen independent variable concepts into seven constructs slightly different from the original schema proposed in figure 2 (chapter 1). Relative high factor scores, more than 0.60 in each factor component, were selected for guiding the modification of the construct as may be necessary; and these are discussed in the following sections.

Table 12
Run B: Factor Analysis Seeking Seven Factors

	Component						
	1	2	3	4	5	6	7
Service-provider was readily available when I contacted the service number.		0.398	0.671	0.160		0.189	0.298
Service-provider seemed to be struggling to find the right words.*		0.111		0.686	0.442	-0.182	0.231
Service-provider understood my urgency.	0.801	0.196	0.240	0.106	0.177		0.142
Service-provider understood my issues clearly.	0.716	0.249	0.257	0.247	0.188	0.116	0.215
Service-provider pronunciation was clear to me.	0.552	0.296	0.204	0.606		0.171	
Service-provider listened to me patiently.	0.524	0.537	0.185	0.181	0.293		0.140
My issues were resolved speedily.	0.490	0.186	0.719		0.161	0.143	
Service-provider seemed to be technically competent.	0.463	0.315	0.632	0.132	0.204		0.149
I was guided by the service-provider as I acted on his/her instructions.	0.439	0.603		0.114	0.301	0.225	0.217

	C	A	D	G	B	F	E
Service-provider spoke at a speed I could understand.	0.399	0.409	0.449	0.477			
I could trust the service-provider to safeguard my personal information.	0.301	0.236	0.299	0.121		0.127	0.807
Service-provider was courteous while providing responses.	0.229	0.796	0.331		0.182		
I felt cheated by the service-provider.*	0.195	0.148	0.216	0.230	0.825		
PC/laptop service-provider was willing to help me.	0.182	0.742	0.350		0.270	0.100	0.145
Service-provider was NOT sincere in his/her efforts to help me.*	0.160	0.323		0.170	0.804		
Service-provider followed-up a few days later to ensure my issue was resolved.	0.143	0.106	0.146			0.946	
Service-provider spoke with a heavy foreign accent. *	-0.136		-0.121	-0.881	-0.180		
Prioritized as per factor scores	C	A	D	G	B	F	E

Extraction Method: Principal Component Analysis.
Rotation Method: Varimax with Kaiser Normalization.
Rotation converged in twelve iterations.

Factor Component 1 (FC1)

Factor scores under FC1 included the variables represented by Q17 (Service-provider understood my issues clearly) and Q23 (Service-provider understood my urgency). These two questions clearly indicated that the customer (respondent) would have liked the service provider to understand not only the specifics of the issue clearly but also the urgency toward a quick resolution. In the theoretical formulation of the study, these two questions had been considered under the constructs of *quality of communication* and *empathy.* There is, thus, a need to arrive at a new construct to reflect the combination of clarity of the issue and a sense of urgency of the respondent toward resolution. Urgency, it could be argued, may be a subconcept when the issue is perceived with clarity by the service provider. Thus, the new construct combining these two concepts will be called *clarity of issue.*

Factor Component 2 (FC2)

There were four variables identified under FC2.

1. Q6 (PC/laptop service-provider was willing to help me).
2. Q7 (Service-provider was courteous while providing responses).
3. Q18 (I was guided by the service-provider as I acted on his/her instructions).
4. Q24 (Service-provider listened to me patiently).

These four variables represent willingness, courtesy, guidance, and patient listening exhibited by the service provider during a service encounter. In the conceptual formulation of the research study, these four variables had been classified under *responsiveness* (Q6 and Q7), *quality of communication* (Q18), and *empathy* (Q24). The grouping of these four variables under FC2 has necessitated rethinking on a new construct. The construct of *compassionate responsiveness* will be used to represent FC2.

Factor Component 3 (FC3)

FC3 had three variables: Q8 (My issues were resolved speedily), Q9 (Service-provider seemed to be technically competent), and Q10 (Service-provider was readily available when I contacted the service number). These three were originally classified under *responsiveness* (Q8 and Q9) and *reliability* (Q10). Timely availability of technical help and speedy resolution being the underlying concepts of FC3, a new construct *technical dependability* will be used to represent FC3.

Factor Component 4 (FC4)

Four variables represented by Q11 (Service-provider spoke at a speed I could understand), Q12 (Service-provider spoke with a heavy foreign accent), Q13 (Service-provider pronunciation was clear to me), and Q16 (Service-provider seemed to be struggling to find the right words) were dominant in FC4. These four variables represented the *quality of communication* in the original schema and covered the concepts related to speed of communication, pronunciation, heavy accent, and vocabulary. The same construct nomenclature *quality of communication* will be retained.

Factor Component 5 (FC5)

FC5 had two components, Q21 (Service-provider was not sincere in his/her efforts to help me) and Q22 (I felt cheated by the service-provider). These two questions had negative connotations, and the scores were reverse coded for proper interpretation. The means of 4.719 and 4.792, respectively, on reversed scores conveyed that the respondents believed that the service providers were largely sincere. The respondents did not feel they were cheated. Both these questions were grouped under the construct of *Service Attitude* in the original schema. Since *Service Attitude* could mean much more (like willingness, patience, and so on) than what is represented by Q21 and Q22, a new nomenclature of *Sincerity* would represent FC5 better.

Factor Component 6 (FC6)

Q19 (Service-provider followed-up a few days later to ensure my issue was resolved) was the only one variable identified in FC6. The question received the lowest mean score mean (2.871) among the seventeen independent variables, indicating that many respondents believed that the service provider did not follow up. This seems to be a definite area of concern. The question was originally classified as *quality of communication*. The nomenclature does not fit Q19 appropriately; a new construct of *follow-up* is introduced to identify the underlying variable of Q19 (and FC6).

Factor Component 7 (FC7)

Only Q27 (I could trust the service-provider to safeguard my personal information) was identified under FC7. Help-desk service providers often have to ask customers for credit card numbers, telephone numbers, and other verifiable personal identification information. Trusting the service provider to safeguard such personal information was important. The question was classified under the broader concept of *ethics* in the original schema, but will better fit with a nomenclature *trust*.

Revised Schema

Based on factor analysis, the same seventeen questions (independent variables) were classified into seven constructs as follows:

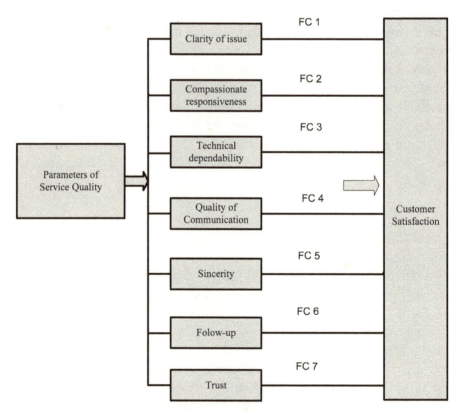

Figure 4. Revised schema of variables

The schema in figure 4 has the factor FC1 through FC7 in serial order, without ascribing priority with respect to the dependent variable, customer satisfaction (Q29). The relative impact of each of these factors (FC1 through FC7) on customer satisfaction will be determined through regression analysis that follows.

Regression Analysis

A univariate linear multiple regression of the seven independent variables (FC1 through FC7) and the dependent variable Q29 (Overall, I was satisfied with the help I received from service provider) was run on SPSS. Regression summary is presented in table 13, with beta coefficients in descending order and reordered list of factors. Results of t-tests on each of the factors with 95% confidence level suggest that all seven factors are significant predictors ($p < 0.001$) of the dependent variable.

Table 13
Regression Summary

	Un-standardized coefficients		Standardized coefficients	t	Sig.	95% Confidence interval for B	
	B	Std. error	Beta			Lower bound	Upper bound
Constant	4.365	0.035		124.450	$p<0.001$	4.296	4.434
FC 2	0.944	0.035	0.598	26.893	$p<0.001$	0.875	1.013
FC 5	0.545	0.035	0.345	15.509	$p<0.001$	0.476	0.614
FC 1	0.469	0.035	0.297	13.371	$p<0.001$	0.400	0.538
FC 3	0.463	0.035	0.293	13.200	$p<0.001$	0.394	0.532
FC 7	0.371	0.035	0.235	10.556	$p<0.001$	0.302	0.440
FC 6	0.320	0.035	0.202	9.104	$p<0.001$	0.251	0.389
FC 4	0.259	0.035	0.164	7.383	$p<0.001$	0.190	0.328

Dependent Variable: Overall, I was satisfied with help I received from service provider.

R	Adjusted R²	Standard error of estimate	Durbin-Watson	F change
0.880	0.770	0.757	2.11	54.51*

*   df1 = 1; df2=458

Durbin-Watson statistic tests for correlations between adjacent residuals; a value at or near 2.00 is considered acceptable. A value lower than 1.00 or higher than 3.00 is considered problematic (Field, 2005). In the present regression, the Durbin-Watson statistic is 2.11 and is considered acceptable.

The F statistic is used to test the overall goodness of fit of the regression model. Theoretically, the hypotheses being tested by the F statistic are as follows:

$$H_0: Y=\beta_0$$
$$H_A: Y= \beta_0 + \beta_1 X_1 + \beta_2 X_2 + \beta_3 X_3 + \beta_4 X_4 + \beta_5 X_5 + \beta_6 X_6 + \beta_7 X_7$$

If the F statistic is not significant, it would mean that the regression did not improve the predictability of Y by the betas. In the regression analyses under consideration, F has a value of 54.51, with a P value of less than 0.001. The null hypothesis above is rejected. The regression betas improve the predictability of the dependent variable, in this case, customer satisfaction.

Table 14 shows revised variable constructs and their components. All the seventeen variables have been used in the seven constructs.

Discussion on Regression Analysis

Results of regression analysis of the survey with 466 respondents suggested that compassionate responsiveness, sincerity of the service provider, clarity of issue, technical dependability, trust, follow-up after a few days, and quality of communication had significant positive effect on customer satisfaction in that service encounter.

1. **Compassionate responsiveness:** The construct includes patient listening, willingness to help, live guidance, and courteous demeanor on the part of the service provider during the service encounter.

Compassionate responsiveness has the highest beta coefficient and contribution to customer satisfaction in the PC help-desk services as suggested by the survey.

Table 14
Revised Variable Constructs

Factor components	Original construct	Revised construct
FC 2		
Service-provider listened to me patiently.	Empathy	
I was guided by the service-provider as I acted on his/her instructions.	Quality of communication	Compassionate responsiveness
Service-provider was courteous while providing responses.	Responsiveness	
PC/laptop service-provider was willing to help me.	Responsiveness	
FC 5		
I felt cheated by the service-provider.*	Service attitude	Sincerity
Service-provider was NOT sincere in his/her efforts to help me.*	Service attitude	
FC 1		
Service-provider understood my urgency.	Empathy	Clarity of issue
Service-provider understood my issues clearly.	Quality of communication	
FC 3		
Service-provider was readily available when I contacted the service number.	Reliability	Technical dependability
My issues were resolved speedily.	Responsiveness	
Service-provider seemed to be technically competent.	Reliability	
FC 7		
I could trust the service-provider to safeguard my personal information.	Ethics	Trust
Service-provider followed-up a few days later to ensure my issue was resolved.	Quality of communication	Follow-up

FC 4		
Service-provider seemed to be struggling to find the right words.*	Quality of communication	
Service-provider pronunciation was clear to me.	Quality of communication	Quality of communication
Service-provider spoke at a speed I could understand.	Quality of communication	
Service-provider spoke with a heavy foreign accent.	Quality of communication	

* These questions had negative connotations and were reverse coded for analysis.

2. **Sincerity:** As the second highest contributor, *sincerity* includes perceived sincerity of the service provider by the customer. The customer should also not get the impression that he/she is being deceived in any manner by the service provider. Genuineness is the underlying theme in the variable.

3. **Clarity of issue:** The variable includes the clear understanding of the issue by the service provider, including the urgency of the issue with regard to the specific customer.

4. **Technical dependability:** Three components make the variable: ready availability of the service provider when contacted, speedy resolution of the issue, and technical competence. While degrees of provider availability and speedy resolution are actually experienced by the customer, technical competence could be an inferred judgment based on the other two components.

5. **Trust:** Initially classified as *ethics,* the variable speaks directly to the confidence the customer has in entrusting personal information to the service provider. The variable did not qualitatively fit into the other six variable concepts. Trustworthiness of the service provider is the underlying concept.

6. **Follow-up:** As stated earlier, follow-up a few days after resolution of the issue had the lowest rating among the mean scores. While initially the concept was covered under the variable *quality of ommunication,* there is a need to classify this as a separate variable for two reasons: time-lapse between the initial service communication and the follow-up, and training implications.

7. **Quality of Communication (QOC):** The components that currently make up QOC as a variable include clear pronunciation, speed of delivery, accent, and vocabulary. The variable ranked last among the seven in terms of beta coefficients and was somewhat of a surprise. Prior opinion cited in chapter 1 seemed to indicate QOC was a more serious problem in affecting customer satisfaction (Fairell, Kaka, and Stürze, 2005).

Revised Schema with Factor Betas

Following the regression analysis, the revised schema is rewritten in the descending order of betas (figure 5).

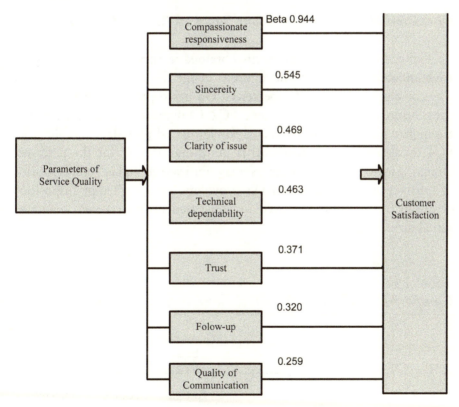

Figure 5. Revised schema with beta rankings

Additional Analysis and Findings—Perceived US and Foreign Providers

The factor analyses and regression analysis discussed so far focused on determinants of customer satisfaction in PC/laptop help-desk services, without making a distinction between perceived US and foreign-service providers. In order to find out the degree of impact of the perceived source of service providers, two separate regressions were carried out on the data grouped into perceived US providers (264 responses) and foreign providers (202 responses) based on the answers to Q30. The seven factors discussed in the previous section were used with slightly different factor loadings in the rotated component matrix.

Discussion of Separate Regressions Based on Perceived Source

Constants and beta coefficients obtained in these separate regressions are compared in table 15 and figure 6 in the descending order of betas. The constants are higher for perceived US-based providers; whereas, beta contribution of all factors, except FC2 (compassionate responsiveness), are higher in the case of perceived foreign-based providers. The beta for FC4 (quality of communication) is more than double for the perceived foreign providers. The constants may indicate a higher predisposition of satisfaction with perceived US providers (or a higher predisposition of dissatisfaction with perceived foreign-based providers) even before an actual service encounter.

Table 15
Comparison of Betas—Perceived Foreign and US Sources

		Un-standardized beta coefficients		
		Foreign	U.S.A.	Difference
Constant		4.399	4.501	-0.1020
FC 1	Clarity of issue	0.841	0.772	0.0690

FC 5	Sincerity	0.634	0.522	0.1120
FC 3	Technical dependability	0.611	0.507	0.1040
FC 4	Quality of communication	0.465	0.207	0.2580
FC 2	Compassionate responsiveness	0.448	0.508	-0.0600
FC 6	Follow-up	0.320	0.259	0.0610
FC 7	Trust	0.295	0.288	0.0070

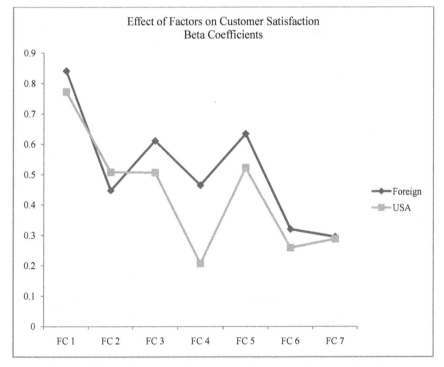

Figure 6. Beta effects based on perceived source of service providers

Detailed SPSS outputs of these two regressions are in appendix K. All factor components in both regressions showed high significance ($p < 0.001$) based on t-tests, suggesting that each of these factor components added significantly to the regression model of the dependent variable—customer satisfaction. Table 16 summarizing ANOVA and F-tests suggested that the regression model was a good fit.

Table 16
F-Tests: Regressions Based on Perceived Foreign and US Sources

R		R Sq.	Adj. R Sq.	Std. error of estimate	Change statistics		Durbin-Watson statistic		
Foreign	U.S.A.				R square change	F change	Sig. F change	Foreign	USA
0.875	0.824	0.766	0.758	0.852	0.032	26.225*	$p < 0.001$	2.082	1.971

*df1=1; df2=194

Table 17 shows the rankings of variable concepts. Irrespective of the source of service, *clarity of issue* and *sincerity* were at the top. In the combined regression, *compassionate responsiveness* had the highest beta (figure 7).

Quality of communication (QOC) had the lowest impact in the case of perceived US-based providers; whereas, the effect QOC has on customer satisfaction seemed to have more than doubled in the case of foreign-based providers. Among the seven factors, beta difference between the perceived service sources was the highest in QOC.

Table 17
Beta Rankings by Perceived Source of Service Provider

Perceived source of service provider	
Foreign	U.S.A.
Clarity of issue	Clarity of issue
Sincerity	Sincerity
Technical dependability	Compassionate responsiveness
Quality of communication	Technical dependability
Compassionate responsiveness	Trust
Follow-up	Follow-up
Trust	Quality of communication

Research Questions and Hypotheses Testing

Since all the seventeen initial variables were also present in the revised configuration, hypotheses were tested in respect of the seven redefined constructs. Table 13 and appendix K, respectively, show the SPSS results for regression for the full data set and for the partial data set representing foreign source only.

1. Compassionate responsiveness

H_0:   Quality of compassionate responsiveness has no effect on customer satisfaction in outsourced help-desk situations.

H_A: Quality of compassionate responsiveness has an effect on customer satisfaction in outsourced help-desk situations.

When regression analysis was conducted for all 466 responses without separating the perceived sources, *compassionate responsiveness* (FC1) as an independent variable had a beta coefficient of 0.944 in the multiple regression with customer satisfaction, the dependent variable. The *t* value for this was 26.893 and was significant at 95% confidence level (table 13). Regression analysis only, with 202 responses that perceived the provider as foreign-based, resulted in a beta of 0.448, *t* value of 7.497, and $p < 0.001$ at 95% confidence level. The null hypothesis was rejected. The conclusion was that there is evidence to suggest that the independent variable construct represented by *compassionate responsiveness* had a positive and significant effect on customer satisfaction (appendix K).

2. Sincerity

H_0:   Sincerity of the service provider has no effect on customer satisfaction in outsourced help-desk situations.

H_A: Sincerity of the service provider has an effect on customer satisfaction in outsourced help-desk situations.

In the combined regression analysis, *sincerity* (FC2) had a coefficient of 0.545, with a *t* value of 15.509 and was significant at 95% confidence level. Considering regression analysis only of perceived foreign-service providers, the beta was 0.634 and still significant ($p < 0.001$) with a t value of 8.648. Null hypothesis was, therefore, rejected. *Sincerity* did have an impact on customer satisfaction.

3. Clarity of issue

H_0:   Clarity of issue has no effect on customer satisfaction in outsourced help-desk situations.

H_A: Clarity of issue has an effect on customer satisfaction in outsourced help-desk situations.

In regression analyses separated by perceived source of service provider, *clarity of issue* had the highest beta (foreign 0.841, USA, 0.772) in both the groups. The t value for the variable in the perceived foreign-based provider data set was 0.841 and was significant ($p < 0.001$) at 95% confidence level.

However, in combined regression analysis reported in table 13, *clarity of issue* had the third place, with a beta of 0.469. The t value for this variable was 13.371 and was significant ($p < 0.001$) at 95% confidence level. The null hypothesis is, therefore, rejected. Based on the evidence, *clarity of issue* (comprising clear understanding by the service provider of the problem and its urgency) had a significant effect on the dependent variable.

4. Technical dependability

H_0:   Technical dependability has no effect on customer satisfaction in outsourced help-desk situations.

H_A: Technical dependability has an effect on customer satisfaction in outsourced help-desk situations.

Both in combined regression analysis (beta 0.463, $t = 13.200$) and in regression analysis of the foreign-provider data set (beta 0.611, $t = 11.049$, and $p < 0.001$), the t values were significant. The null hypothesis is rejected, and there is support for the alternate hypothesis that technical dependability, as expressed through timely availability of technical help and speedy resolution, has significant effect on customer satisfaction.

5. Trust

H_0:   Trust in the service provider has no effect on customer satisfaction in outsourced help-desk situations.

H_A: Trust in the service provider has an effect on customer satisfaction in outsourced help-desk situations.

Data analyzed in the research study pointed to trust as the confidence of the customer in entrusting personal information to the service provider. Regression analyses showed betas of 0.371 (combined) and 0.295 (foreign provider), with t values of 10.556 and 5.606 respectively. Both t values were significant ($p < 0.001$) at 95% confidence level, rejecting null hypothesis, and supporting the alternate hypothesis.

6. Follow-up

H_0:   Follow-up by the service provider has no effect on customer satisfaction in outsourced help-desk situations.

H_A: Follow-up by the service provider has an effect on customer satisfaction in outsourced help-desk situations.

The construct *follow-up* had a beta of 0.320 in both the regression analyses (combined and foreign). The corresponding t values were 9.104 and 5.121 and were significant ($p < 0.001$) at 95% confidence level, rejecting the null hypothesis. The construct *follow-up* has a significant effect on customer satisfaction, the dependent variable.

7. Quality of communication (QOC)

H_0:   Quality of communication of the service provider has no effect on customer satisfaction in outsourced help-desk situations.

H_A: Quality of communication of the service provider has an effect on customer satisfaction in outsourced help-desk situations.

Although there were indications in literature that quality of communication was an important factor in customer satisfaction of outsourced help-desk services, beta coefficient for perceived foreign-based providers was 0.465, ranked fifth among the seven variable constructs. The beta for QOC in the combined regression analyses was ranked lowest at 0.259. Results from t-tests showed t values of 5.89 (foreign) and 7.383 (combined), both being significant ($p < 0.001$) at 95% confidence level, so null hypothesis was rejected and alternate hypothesis supported.

Each of the seven independent variable constructs has a significant impact on the dependent variable customer satisfaction in perceived outsourced PC/laptop help-desk services. Further, F-test for goodness of fit showed that the combined regression model had an F statistic value of 54.515, R-value of 0.880, and a significance of 7.332E-13, indicating the model with seven independent variable constructs was a good fit for the predictive relationship of customer satisfaction.

Additional Comments on Analyses

While analyzing and testing several variables, the possibility of type I error (false positive) is inevitable by design and has to be considered carefully. Multiple variables could raise the potential of type I errors if the survey is not conducted and analyzed appropriately.

Firstly, the degree of type I error can be reduced if randomness of probabilities in the distribution is achieved. This would require adequate sample size and random selection of respondents. In the research study, the theoretical sample size requirement was 385, 400 random respondents were sought at a minimum, and in the end, 466 usable responses were analyzed. This would contribute to controlling and reducing any false positives.

Further in the research study, a 95% confidence was used throughout. However, the seventeen variables were also tested at 99% level to make certain that type I errors were minimized in the process of hypotheses testing. All but one of the P values obtained in the analyses were lower than 0.002, and one P value was near 0.009, thus strongly supporting the true rejection of null hypotheses in all seventeen variables. In the research study, therefore, the potential for false positives (type I error) was extremely low.

Chapter Summary

After arriving at a research methodology and design as explained in chapter 3, data collection and analyses were carried out as described in the chapter. The survey instrument was externally validated for content and concept using the interrater agreement (IRA) method. After minor modifications, a pilot survey was launched to a random representative sample. The process proceeded without further problems, and the respondent data seemed to indicate that the instrument could yield significant results toward addressing the purpose and research questions in the study.

Given the target population as US residents who had purchased PCs/laptops less than a year ago, a suitable database was procured, and the main survey was fielded. A total of 1,263 e-mail surveys were sent, and 466 complete responses were received. Out of twenty-three independent variables, six were removed because of multicollinearity. The data for the remaining seventeen variables were analyzed using comparison of means, factor analyses, and regression analyses.

Seven factor components were identified and the compositions of these were found to be slightly different from the theoretical combinations presented in figure 1. The new factor components (or independent variable constructs) were compassionate responsiveness, sincerity, clarity of issue, technical dependability, trust, follow-up, and quality of communication. Research hypotheses corresponding to the seven variable constructs were tested using two-tailed t-tests at 95% and all the seven variables were found to be significant ($p < 0.001$) as predictors of customer satisfaction, the dependent variable.

In order to assess the impact of perceived foreign-based services on customer satisfaction and to verify the determinants of customer satisfaction, two additional regression analyses were conducted by grouping the data under perceived US-based and foreign-based service providers. These regression analyses also showed that all the seven constructs were still significant in each group although the rankings were slightly different. The following chapter will discuss study findings, presenting conclusions that follow from them, recommendations to leadership of firms involved with PC/laptop customer service, suggestions for future research, and reflections on the study process.

CHAPTER 5

CONCLUSIONS AND RECOMMENDATIONS

Use of external agents for servicing customers, referred to as outsourcing, has grown in recent years. The strategy of outsourcing had led US firms to foreign-based service providers, and such moves have been justified based on cost or competitive advantage. Such outsourcing is expected to grow substantially in future years. A conference board survey of fifty-two different types of companies in the United States and Europe indicated that 79% of them outsourced help-desk processes to overseas providers and that information technology processes were outsourced three times more than any other functional services (Schniederjans and Cao, 2006). Barthelemy (2003) estimated that 58% of the organizations would outsource their informational technology services by 2010.

Purpose of This Study: Revisited

Notwithstanding the explosive growth, or perhaps because of it, there were concerns about the outsourced services. American Customer Satisfaction Index (ACSI), published by the University of Michigan, indicated that the service quality in the PC industry was almost 10% below the average of other consumer durables; the lower service quality was attributed, in part, to customer frustrations with PC call centers and to the complex nature of the PC products (as cited in Koprovski, 2006). Marshall and Heffes (2005), citing a report by Deloitte Consulting, indicated an undercurrent of customer dissatisfaction in outsourced services. Panther and Farquhar (2004) stressed the monitoring of customer satisfaction and an understanding of the reasons of dissatisfaction in order to prevent loss of customers in the service industries. A study of the determinants of customer satisfaction related to outsourced help-desk services in the PC/laptop industry was, therefore, necessary and timely. The purpose of the quantitative study was to identify the determinants of customer satisfaction and, in doing so, determine the relationship between several customer service factors and customer satisfaction of perceived outsourced help-desk services in the PC industry.

Research Approach and Design

An examination of customer satisfaction literature since 1988 showed that many studies used gap analysis (as seen in the popular SERVQUAL and its modified approaches) where customer expectations and service fulfillment were assessed in measuring the degree of satisfaction. In the current research study, customer satisfaction was defined as a postservice evaluative judgment of a service encounter resulting in a pleasurable end state based on a combined assessment of the performance of service factors that constituted that service. Keeping the definition in focus, the current research study has included concepts drawn not only from the marketing perspectives of customer satisfaction, but also from communication, ethics, and language-based research literature.

Survey and Analysis of Data

The survey population was US-based customers of PC and laptop products. A sample size of four hundred usable responses was determined adequate. A survey instrument with twenty-three Likert-type questions and three demographic questions was pilot tested to thirty respondents after obtaining an interrater agreement of about 87% on the survey instrument. Minor technical issues were resolved, and the main survey was fielded via e-mail to 1,263 potential respondents. The survey questionnaire (appendix A) had been designed with a skip-logic question to obtain informed consent from the respondents. There were 466 completed responses with no missing data, representing a response rate of 36.90%. The data received were coded for analysis by SPSS software.

Subsequent to factor analyses and regression analyses of the 466 responses, seventeen variables were found to be significant, but showed different grouping patterns in terms of factor components. After examining the major components of each of the factors, the same seventeen variables were grouped into seven slightly modified constructs in a revised schema (see figure 5). Since the revised nomenclatures of the constructs reflected the responses in the survey, these revised constructs could be concluded as a more realistic representation than the initial theoretical schema. Both the initial and revised versions are shown in figure 7.

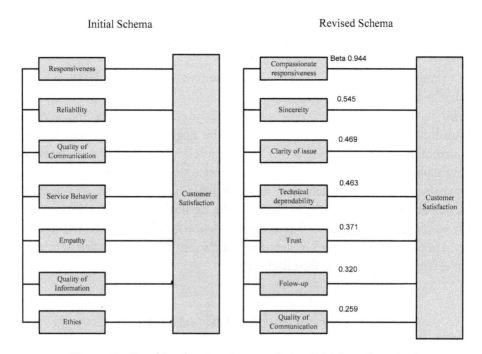

Figure 7. Combined regression analysis: initial and revised schema of variable constructs

Research Questions Answered

The focus of the research study was to find the determinants of customer satisfaction in perceived outsourced help-desk services in the PC industry. Specifically, the study was used to find whether responsiveness, reliability, quality of communication, quality of information, service attitude, empathy, and ethics had any effect on customer satisfaction in perceived outsourced help-desk services in the PC industry. These seven constructs were made up of seventeen independent variables.

All seventeen variables in the research study were found to have significant impact on customer satisfaction in the area of PC help-desk services; however, the groupings of these seventeen variables produced seven slightly different, but better-defined constructs. The seven refined variable constructs were compassionate responsiveness, sincerity, clarity of issue, technical dependability, trust, follow-up, and quality of communication. During the conceptualization phase of the research study, variable constructs like responsiveness and reliability had necessarily to be based on prior research literature. The finding that the final variable constructs are slightly different leads to the conclusion that PC help-desk services, in fact, need a different approach to the sustenance and improvement of customer satisfaction. These seven new constructs were also found statistically significant in predicting customer satisfaction in the perceived outsourced help-desk services in the PC industry. These seven constructs, therefore, are concluded to be the seven determinants of customer satisfaction in outsourced PC help-desk services. The findings are discussed in following sections.

Findings and Conclusions—General

The general nature of the problem that prompted the research study was the customer dissatisfaction in perceived outsourced services for US-based PC/laptop customers. A general finding of the research study was that customer satisfaction with perceived foreign-service providers was significantly lower than customer satisfaction with perceived US-service providers. The evidence of lower customer satisfaction in foreign-service providers is consistent with previous reports from Koprovski (2006), Marshall and Heffes (2005), and Mello (2007). The latest overall score of American Customer Satisfaction Index (ACSI) for the PC industry published in August 2008 also shows a slippage from seventy-five to seventy-four between August 2007 and August 2008. While the underlying cause of the latest slippage has been attributed to changes in PC operating systems in non-Mac platforms, the effect could be an increase in customer calls to the help-desk services (Fornell, 2008). The current research study of determinants of customer satisfaction of help-desk services in the PC industry, it could be concluded, was well warranted and timely.

Findings and Conclusions—Determinants of Customer Satisfaction

Based on the research and analyses presented so far, the following seven variable constructs emerged as the determinants of customer satisfaction in outsourced PC/laptop help-desk services. These findings and their implications are discussed in the following sections.

Compassionate Responsiveness

The variable was found to represent a combination of responsiveness and empathy components. In the theoretical formulation of the model leading to the research study, the variable was named *responsiveness* and was composed of willingness to help, accompanied by courtesy, availability, quick response, and a speedy resolution of the customer's concerns based on the concepts used in SERVQUAL and modifications thereof (Parasuraman et al., 1988; Parasuraman, Zeithaml, and Malhotra, 2005). In addition, in the initial model, *empathy* was regarded as a separate variable. Empathy was a set of expressed attitudes that covered six aspects: expressions of caring remarks, consideration for customer's time and urgency, ability to listen patiently, trustworthiness, friendliness, and attentiveness (Parasuraman et al., 1988).

In the current research study, courtesy and willingness to help were found to be significant variables, along with patient listening and active guidance. The finding reinforces the research of Chen (2005) who had observed that many service encounters in the age of technology were in the nature of self-service technology (SST) encounters. Chen had concluded that the determinants of customer satisfaction in the SST and face-to-face interpersonal encounters were different. The current finding regarding active guidance by the service provider supports the conclusion that service encounters in the PC help-desk services often have an element of SST at the customer's end. Another conclusion from the finding is that patient listening by service providers and active guidance of the customer are essential parts of being responsive. A further conclusion is that a new nomenclature *compassionate responsiveness* is necessary to represent the variable better. Compassionate responsiveness was also found to have the highest impact on customer satisfaction in the combined (perceived foreign and US-based providers) analysis of PC help-desk services. Recommended action to the PC industry would be to find training approaches to blend empathy and action components of responsiveness at the service providers' end.

Sincerity

Previous research had considered sincerity as a part of the construct of reliability (Parasuraman et al., 1988; Parasuraman et al., 2005) or part of service attitude (Winsted, 2000). However, the finding in the current study on PC help-desk services was that sincerity as a variable consisted of two specific aspects—a genuine approach to assist the customer and an assurance that the customer was not being deceived. The finding about the expectation of nondeception confirms observations of service encounters by Roman (2007).

Sincerity as a determinant of customer satisfaction with PC help-desk services was additionally found to have the second highest impact on customer satisfaction. Sincerity, as explained here, was a combination of a genuine attitude and of correctly exuding the same to assure the customer. A conclusion of the finding was that service providers needed to be trained to show genuineness and to assure that customers were not being cheated. It is recommended that customer awareness and confidence building measures be vigorously implemented.

Clarity of Issue

Two components were found to define clarity of issue as a determinant of customer satisfaction: the ability of the service provider to understand the customer's problems without ambiguity and the ability to understand their urgency. The findings showed that clarity of issue was a distinct and significant factor in influencing customer satisfaction of PC help-desk services. In fact, in the analysis of survey data separated by source of service (perceived foreign and US providers), clarity of issue was found as the top influencer in each of the groups.

In addition, the service provider has to understand the urgency of the solution to the customer. Boshoff and Staude (2003) had concluded that satisfaction was influenced by communication that included clarity of communication and service provider's ability to understand the customer's issues. Although Boshoff and Staude's research had focused on service-recovery situations, a similar finding emerged in the current study of PC help-desk services. In conclusion, high priority should be placed by the service provider on understanding the nature of the customer's problem and its urgency. Understanding the clarity and urgency were, in turn, found to be well related to technical competence and dependability discussed later. Service providers, both US and foreign, should be trained in asking appropriate probing questions to understand the issue and the urgency of its resolution to the customer.

Technical Dependability

Analyses of the survey data specifically revealed that ready availability when called, technical competence of the service provider, and speed of resolution of the issue were three components of a variable that could be named *technical dependability*. Technical dependability was found to have significant impact on customer satisfaction in PC help-desk services. Earlier research literature had covered technical competence, dependability, and speed of resolution under reliability and responsiveness (Parasuraman et al., 1988; Parasuraman, Zeithaml, and Malhotra, 2005). The finding in the current research study of PC help-desk services, while generally supporting previous research, suggests a regrouping of the three components of speed, availability, and competence under one construct of technical dependability.

An additional finding among these three factors was that technical competence and speed of resolution were positively correlated, leading to a conclusion that effective service providers had to be technically competent. While this might not seem to be a new revelation, recent concerns of customers were mainly related to PC operating systems (Fornell, 2008), leading to a conclusion that there was some urgency to the improvement of technical dependability as defined in the section. Another conclusion is that mere availability of the service provider on call was not enough to improve customer satisfaction in PC help-desk services; availability on call had to be accompanied by technical competence and speedy resolution. Keeping pace with continuously changing PC technology could be a challenge to trainers of service providers. It is recommended that greater attention should be paid to train the trainer continually to update technological competencies at the service provider end.

Trust

Trust was brought out in the current study represented confidence or faith that the service provider could be relied upon to safeguard personal information of the customer. Trust was found to be a stand-alone variable that significantly influenced customer satisfaction in PC help-desk services. Earlier research (Parasuraman et al., 1988) had considered elements of trust as part of reliability or dependability. Bauer, Falk, and Hammerschmidt (2006) had expanded the reliability construct to include confidentiality. In a study of customer satisfaction of Internet banking services in Hong Kong, Liao and Cheung (2008) had also suggested that privacy and security were measures of reliability. Current findings, while supporting these previous studies, lead to the conclusion that trust factor with regard to personal information significantly affect customer satisfaction in PC help-desk services. A conclusion from a managerial perspective is that prior breaches of security and privacy at specific service providers should be taken into account before awarding them to outsourcing contracts. Continuous monitoring of compliance to privacy and security standards is also recommended at the service provider's end.

Follow-Up

Analyses of data in the current research brought out follow-up as a distinct variable with significant impact on customer satisfaction with PC help-desk services. One finding was that the survey question relating to follow-up received the lowest score among all the tested independent variables, indicating there was a definite need to improve this aspect. An additional finding was that follow-up was a significant area of concern in both US-based and foreign-based service providers. These findings support earlier research related to customer satisfaction where follow-through had been considered as a part of service reliability (Boshoff and Staude, 2003). A logical conclusion is that in order to improve customer satisfaction, PC help-desk service providers have to contact the serviced customer and ensure that the resolution was satisfactory. While additional studies may have to be undertaken to arrive at the nature and timing of such follow-up, firms should be able to call back the customer or send an e-mail easily.

Such follow-up is recommended as it would result in improved customer satisfaction.

Quality of Communication

Specific to PC help-desk services, the finding was that quality of communication (QOC) was a significant factor influencing customer satisfaction. Further, QOC was found to be made up of four components: proper pronunciation, good vocabulary, appropriate speed of communication, and moderation of heavy accent. Clarity of speech, as defined, was found to be more important to the customer than fluency in English. These findings support earlier research by others in the area of customer service and communication (Boshoff and Staude, 2003; Matsuura, Chiba, and Fujieda, 1999). One conclusion that emanated from the current study was that QOC in the PC help-desk services retained only speech-related components of communication like pronunciation, speed, accent, and vocabulary while action-related components like live guidance and follow-up were better left to be grouped under other variables like technical dependability and follow-up. An additional conclusion was that such delineation was useful from a managerial perspective in that a verbal communication expert could be used to give focused training on aspects of vocabulary, speed of delivery, and accent.

Related to QOC, another finding was that between perceived US—and foreign-based service providers, heavily accented speech had the highest difference in mean scores. Analyses also showed that a slight negative correlation existed between speed of resolution and heavy accent. These findings lead to the conclusion that improvement in the speed of resolution (and, therefore, customer satisfaction) was attainable by minimizing the heavily accented speech during a service encounter. Although in the combined rankings the effect of QOC was the lowest, there was a much higher impact of QOC on customer satisfaction in perceived foreign-based providers compared to that with US-based providers of PC help-desk services. The conclusion is that a definite need exists to remedy issues related to speed of delivery of speech, heavy accents, pronunciation, and vocabulary among foreign-based PC help-desk service providers.

Additional Findings Related to Perceived Foreign Service Providers

An additional finding that came out of the study was that a predisposition of higher satisfaction existed with perceived US-based providers (or a predisposition of dissatisfaction with perceived foreign-based providers) even if there was no influence of any of the seven determinants. This leads to a conclusion that an improvement in customer satisfaction across the board in PC help-desk services would be achieved if the predisposition of customer dissatisfaction with perceived foreign-based service providers is reduced. Public relations and marketing efforts are recommended as means to improve customer awareness and confidence about the quality and monitoring of outsourced help-desk services.

When the seven determinants were compared for perceived foreign, US, and combined (US plus foreign) providers, a different ranking was found as shown in table 18. A conclusion from this is that the focus in terms of training, management, and measurement of help-desk service employees has to be different for foreign-based providers and US-based providers.

Recommendations to Leadership

During the period 2005-2007, bad experiences with call centers had cost millions of dollars to the PC industry, forcing some firms to relocate overseas call centers back to USA (Alster, 2005; Fairell, Kaka, and Stürze, 2005; Scott, 2007). Poor communication skills, subpar practices, corruption, data theft, and privacy concerns were serious issues; any one of these aspects could affect customer satisfaction (Beshouri, Farrell, and Umezawa, 2005). There was also evidence to suggest that customer satisfaction was lower in outsourced help-desk services in the PC/laptop industry (Koprovski, 2006). Several authors have linked increases in customer satisfaction to long-term profitability and competitive advantage. Decrease in customer satisfaction has been linked to reduction in the return on investment (Gupta and Zeithaml, 2006). Notwithstanding such concerns, outsourcing of services, especially in the IT help-desk services sector, continued to grow vigorously, bringing a level of urgency to the understanding of the underlying components of customer satisfaction in the area.

Table 18
Ranking of Determinants: Perceived Sources

Perceived source of service provider		
Foreign	U.S.A.	Combined
Clarity of issue	Clarity of issue	Compassionate responsiveness
Sincerity	Sincerity	Sincerity
Technical dependability	Compassionate responsiveness	Clarity of issue
Quality of communication	Technical dependability	Technical dependability
Compassionate responsiveness	Trust	Trust
Follow-up	Follow-up	Follow-up
Trust	Quality of communication	Quality of communication

In addition, the linkage between customer satisfaction on the one hand and competitive advantage and profitability on the other is an established fact. Research by Luo and Bhattacharya (2006) and by Lee and Hwan (2005) determined that customer satisfaction increased profitability and market value. Smith and Wright (2004) studied customer satisfaction and loyalty in the PC industry and concluded that high customer loyalty resulted in a competitive advantage in the PC industry.

Pursuant to the current research study, the principal recommendation to PC industry leadership is to take cognizance of each of these seven determinants with a view to improve customer satisfaction with help-desk services. A recommended first step for the leadership is to conduct customer satisfaction surveys using the seven determinants identified in the study, followed by an analysis of strengths and weaknesses in each determinant specific to the PC firm. A training program should then be instituted aimed at improving the attitudes and skills of the service providers.

It is recommended that the seventeen concepts that make up the seven determinants of customer satisfaction be used as training components by leadership of the industry in three broad categories: attitudinal competency, technical competency, and communication competency (table 19).

Table 19
Training Focus

Attitudinal competency	Technical competency	Communication competency
Willingness to help	Guidance to customer	Ready availability on the help-line
Patient listening	Clear understanding of the problem	Trustworthiness with personal information
Courtesy	Understanding of urgency	Follow-up after resolution
Genuineness	Technical expertise	Proper pronunciation
Nondeception	Speedy resolution	Good vocabulary
		Appropriate speed of communication
		Moderation of heavy accent

It is further recommended that effectiveness of such training be measured by longitudinal studies of customer satisfaction on the customer side and through longitudinal psychometric measurements of the service providers. A detailed discussion on these is beyond the scope of the study.

Suggestions for Future Research

While the research study has achieved its primary objective of identifying the determinants of customer satisfaction in outsourced PC help-desk services, there are areas that could be addressed by future research studies:

1. The study was used to focus on one segment of the help-desk services—the PC industry. The seven factors identified in the study are mostly generic in concept and could possibly see use in other areas of outsourced help-desk services. Additional research could be conducted to verify the applicability of the present findings to

help-desk services in other sectors like banking, insurance, travel, and finance.

2. Customer differences in terms of ethnicity, product knowledge, education, technical skill, mother tongue, languages spoken, and other customer demographics were not considered as variables in the study. Future studies could incorporate customer demographic and psychographic characteristics also as independent or intervening variables influencing the seven determinants of customer satisfaction.

3. A key assumption of the study was about the perceived source of help-desk services. The survey depended on the respondent's perception of the source of service, quite simply because the survey was external to a specific PC maker. There was no way (for an outsider) of knowing whether a particular respondent was, in fact, served by someone overseas. The study can be improved upon and verified by PC manufacturers or service providers by studying two specific customer databases: one known to have been served only by foreign providers and the other only by US-based providers.

4. Improvement of customer satisfaction through training (focused on the seven determinants) can be ascertained by a longitudinal study on the service provider's side. Such a study would assure leadership of firms that the training efforts were in fact effective.

5. A predisposition of lower customer satisfaction was seen in the case of foreign-based service providers, even without the seven determinants. Future research should study the reasons for such predisposition and remedies thereof.

6. The research study was specific to the customers in the United States of America. Similar studies could be undertaken in other countries that outsource their services.

Author's Reflections

The quality of outsourced services in various business sectors and the resultant customer dissatisfaction with such services have been publicly expressed concerns. The researcher has personally seen the mushrooming growth of call centers in India and is aware of the extraordinary length some call centers go to train help-desk service providers and to keep their morale high. Given the researcher's extensive global business background, the continued growth of outsourced services, especially to countries whose native language was not English, raised concerns in the researcher's mind.

1. Was customer satisfaction being shortchanged in pursuit of low-cost services?
2. Was proper training given in all aspects of customer service?
3. Were language and communication serious issues, or were they just being blown out of proportion by the media?
4. Was customer dissatisfaction more pronounced in certain industries?
5. How different were the satisfaction levels provided by different service providers in the same country? In different countries?
6. Were foreign-service providers getting proper feedback in order to improve their services?
7. How can service providers across borders attain consistency?

Answers to these questions would probably take several research studies—possibly cross-country studies spread over many months. Of immediate interest to the researcher was to explore the determinants of customer satisfaction that could lead to other studies and possibly answer some of the questions. The researcher's sales and marketing background probably influenced the initial affinity to the area of customer satisfaction. Troubles with outsourced services of Dell computers had made the news, and at the same time, PC companies in the US did not fare too well on the ACSI. PC industry became the natural choice of study for the researcher.

While outsourcing to foreign countries had been argued as an inevitable strategy for retaining competitive and cost advantages, the researcher saw a significant gap in terms of empirical research assessing the customer side of outsourcing. There was probably an expectation on the part of the researcher that such an investigation would show outsourced services as of being lower quality and worthy of being doubted, if not shunned, by US consumers. The researcher's expectation was also that the study would probably show quality of communication (QOC) (related to pronunciation, accent, and vocabulary) to be a serious concern. While QOC was found to be a significant factor, the researcher was mildly surprised that QOC's impact was much less than that of other factors.

During the research formulation phase, an early concern for the researcher was on the means to identify and survey customers that were served only by foreign-based providers. Despite the researcher's contacts with some PC companies, the demographic set seemed to be not easily available to researchers outside the firms. A solution adopted by the researcher was to study provider sources as perceived by the customers themselves.

The researcher believes the study has made a valuable contribution to the area of customer satisfaction in outsourced services and filled a gap in terms of assessing the determinants of customer satisfaction. Many suggestions have been made for potential future studies that may help add to the knowledge.

Summary and Conclusions

The concluding chapter of the research study revisited the purpose of the study and discussed the findings and conclusions of the empirical analyses presented earlier in chapter 4. The successful completion of the study has brought a fresh understanding of the determinants of customer satisfaction specific to perceived outsourced help-desk services in the PC industry from an external researcher's perspective and filled a knowledge gap in the area. Seven significant determinants of customer satisfaction and seventeen variable concepts were identified as related to PC help-desk services. These seven determinants of customer satisfaction were compassionate responsiveness, sincerity, clarity of issue, technical dependability, trust, follow-up, and quality of communication. Specific recommendations were made on each of these variables. Corporate training in three competency areas—attitudinal competency, technical competency, and communication competency—was recommended.

The findings, conclusions, and recommendations of the study are expected to guide the leaders of the PC industry and their overseas service providers in improving customer satisfaction and long-term competitive advantage. A recommended next step for the PC industry is to conduct similar studies from within the firm where more specific customer data may be available. Several future studies in the area have been suggested. In the end, the findings of the research study will benefit both firms and their stakeholders through better service and higher customer satisfaction.

APPENDIX A

SURVEY INSTRUMENT

Dear Respondent,

As part of my doctoral research study at the University of Phoenix, I am conducting a survey that investigates customer satisfaction of help-desk services in the personal computing (PC) industry. The study is expected to bring out factors that determine customer satisfaction in the PC industry especially as related to outsourced help-desk services.

If you had called any PC help-line in 2008 seeking assistance with your PC or Laptop computer, I shall appreciate your completing the attached survey. Please answer all the 28 questions to the best of your ability. The survey is voluntary and does not ask you for any personally identifiable information. The survey will take approximately 15 minutes and may be completed anytime within two weeks. All responses will be kept confidential.

The data collected from the survey will be stored by the researcher on an external hard drive not connected to the Internet. The data will be stored for three years from the closing date of the survey and will then be destroyed by the researcher. Nobody other than the researcher will have access to the survey data.

Thank you again for your cooperation.

Vellore Sunder
vsunder@e-mail.phoenix.edu
University of Phoenix Online-School of Advanced Studies

CONSENT

By giving consent, I acknowledge that I understand the nature of the study, the potential risks to me as a participant, and the means by which my identity will be kept confidential. By clicking the first button below, I am indicating that I am 18 years old or older and that I give my permission to serve voluntarily as a participant in the study described.

☐   I AGREE

> No personally identifiable information has been sought in the survey. All responses will be kept strictly confidential.

SURVEY

1. Gender   ☐ Male   ☐ Female
2. Type of PC you called help-desk about   ☐ Apple   ☐ Dell   ☐ HP/Compaq
                                          ☐ IBM   ☐ Gateway ☐ Sony
                                          ☐ Toshiba ☐ Others
3. Approximately how long ago did you contact your PC help-desk service?
                       ☐   Less than three months ago
                       ☐   More than three months ago
                       ☐   I do not remember

GO TO NEXT PAGE

		STRONGLY DISAGREE					STRONGLY AGREE
		1	2	3	4	5	6
4	Service-provider was willing to help me.	☐	☐	☐	☐	☐	☐
5	Service-provider was courteous in his/her responses.	☐	☐	☐	☐	☐	☐
6	My issues were resolved speedily.	☐	☐	☐	☐	☐	☐
7	Service-provider seemed to be technically competent.	☐	☐	☐	☐	☐	☐
8	Service-provider was readily available when I contacted the service number.	☐	☐	☐	☐	☐	☐
9	Service-provider spoke at a speed I could keep pace with.	☐	☐	☐	☐	☐	☐
10	Service-provider spoke with a heavy foreign accent.	☐	☐	☐	☐	☐	☐
11	Service-provider's pronunciation was clear to me.	☐	☐	☐	☐	☐	☐
12	The instructions given by the service-provider were clear.	☐	☐	☐	☐	☐	☐
13	Service-provider spoke in fluent English.	☐	☐	☐	☐	☐	☐
14	Service-provider seemed to be struggling to find the right words.	☐	☐	☐	☐	☐	☐
15	Service-provider seemed to understand my issues clearly.	☐	☐	☐	☐	☐	☐
16	I was guided by the service-provider as I continued to work on the issue.	☐	☐	☐	☐	☐	☐
17	Service-provider followed-up to ensure my issue was resolved.	☐	☐	☐	☐	☐	☐
18	Service provider had a friendly attitude.	☐	☐	☐	☐	☐	☐
19	Service-provider was not sincere in his/her efforts to help me.	☐	☐	☐	☐	☐	☐
20	I felt cheated by the service-provider	☐	☐	☐	☐	☐	☐
21	Service-provider understood my urgency.	☐	☐	☐	☐	☐	☐
22	He/she listened to me patiently	☐	☐	☐	☐	☐	☐

		STRONGLY DISAGREE					STRONGLY AGREE
24	The information given to me was relevant in resolving my issue.	☐	☐	☐	☐	☐	☐
25	I could trust the service-provider to safeguard my personal information	☐	☐	☐	☐	☐	☐
26	Service-provider was caring.	☐	☐	☐	☐	☐	☐
27	Overall, I was satisfied with the service.	☐	☐	☐	☐	☐	☐

28. I think the service-provider was based in   ☐   U.S.A   ☐   Overseas

END OF SURVEY

Thank you for participating in the survey. All responses will be kept strictly confidential.

APPENDIX B

INTERRATER REVIEW FORMAT

A	B	C	D	E	F		
	Statement	Area	Components	Is the statement in column B clear to you?		Does the statement pertain generally to the area in column C?	
				YES	NO	YES	NO
4	Service-provider was willing to help me.	Responsiveness	Willingness to help				
5	Service-provider was courteous in his/her responses.	Responsiveness	Courtesy				
6	My issues were resolved speedily.	Responsiveness	Speedy resolution				
7	Service-provider seemed to be technically competent.	Reliability	Technical competence				
8	Service-provider was readily available when I contacted the service number.	Reliability	Availability on call				
9	Service-provider spoke at a speed I could keep pace with.	Quality of communication	Acceptable speed of delivery of speech				

10	Service-provider spoke with a heavy foreign accent.	Quality of communication	Accent
11	Service-provider's pronunciation was clear to me.	Quality of communication	Clarity of pronunciation
12	The instructions given by the service-provider were clear.	Quality of communication	Clarity of instruction
13	Service-provider spoke in fluent English.	Quality of communication	Fluency in English
14	Service-provider seemed to be struggling to find the right words.	Quality of communication	Vocabulary
15	Service-provider understood my issues clearly.	Quality of communication	Ability to understand customer
16	I was guided by the service-provider as I continued to work on the issue.	Quality of communication	Live guidance through process
17	Service-provider followed-up to ensure my issue was resolved.	Quality of communication	Follow-through
18	Service-provider had a friendly attitude	Service attitude	Congeniality
19	Service-provider was not sincere in his/her efforts to help me.	Service attitude	Genuineness
20	I felt cheated by the service-provider.	Service attitude	Concern
21	Service-provider understood my urgency.	Empathy	Consideration
22	He/she listened to me patiently.	Empathy	Listening patiently
23	I could trust the service provider to solve my issue.	Empathy	Trustworthiness

24	The information given to me was relevant in resolving my issue.	Quality of Information	Relevance
25	I could trust the service-provider to safeguard my personal information.	Ethics	Security expectations
26	The service-provider was caring.	Ethics	Nondeception
27	Overall, I was satisfied with the service.	Overall satisfaction	
28	I think the service-provider was based in U.S.A OVERSEAS	Perceived source	

APPENDIX C

MODIFICATIONS TO SURVEY INSTRUMENT

Question	Comments/Suggestions from Reviewers	Changes, if any
Service-provider was willing to help me.	Which service provider?	PC/laptop service-provider was willing to help me.
Service-provider was courteous while providing responses.	courteous "in" responses or when providing responses?	Changed to "courteous while providing responses."
My issues were resolved speedily.	Is "speedily" really a word?	Checked, and original phrase retained.
Service-provider seemed to be technically competent.		
Service-provider was readily available when I contacted the service number.	What is "readily available?"	None. Readily available means available at the other end of the line when called.
Service-provider spoke at a speed I could keep pace with.	Do we keep pace with others who speak? Or, is it more related to speaking at a pace that allows the individual to understand what is being said?	"Keep pace with" to be changed to "understand."

Service-provider spoke with a heavy foreign accent.	How are you defining "heavy?" Can you or should you just say "with a foreign accent?"	Checked, and original phrase retained.
Service-provider's pronunciation was clear to me. The instructions given by the service-provider were clear. Service-provider spoke in fluent English. Service-provider seemed to be struggling to find the right words. Service-provider understood my issues clearly.		
I was guided by the service-provider as I continued to work on the issue	Concerned not everyone will understand this the same way	Changed to: "I was guided by the service-provider as I acted on his/her instructions."
Service-provider followed-up a few days later to ensure my issue was resolved. Service-provider had a friendly attitude Service-provider was not sincere in his/her efforts to help me. I felt cheated by the service-provider. Service-provider understood my urgency.		
He/she listened to me patiently.	Why he/she?	Service-provider listened to me patiently.
I could trust the service provider to solve my issue. The information given to me was relevant in resolving my issue.		

I could trust the service-provider to safeguard my personal information.		
The service-provider was caring.	Should this be classified or ethics or empathy?	Empathy could be fine; subset of ethics. No change in the question.
Overall, I was satisfied with help I received from service provider		
I think the service-provider was based in		
	Based in "Overseas" awkward.	Changed to "A Foreign Country"
USA OVERSEAS		

APPENDIX D

FINAL SURVEY INSTRUMENT

Dear Respondent,

Attached is a survey questionnaire about **Customer Satisfaction of PC/laptop Help-desk services** focused on outsourced services. This is part of my doctoral study at the University of Phoenix. Results of the research study can have an effect on help-desk services for computer users.

The survey is voluntary, will take less than 10 minutes, and does not ask you for any personally identifiable information. All responses will be kept confidential, and data collected from the survey will be destroyed by the researcher after three years.

Your help with the survey is greatly appreciated.

Thank you.

V. Sunder
University of Phoenix Online-School of Advanced Studies

CONSENT: I understand the nature of the study and the means by which my identity will be kept confidential.

By clicking the AGREE button below I am indicating that I am 18 years old or older and that I give my permission to serve voluntarily as a participant in the study described.

☐ **AGREE**   ☐ **DISAGREE**

1. Gender

☐ MALE   ☐ FEMALE

2. **Type of PC/laptop you called help-desk about (Check all that apply)**

☐ APPLE ☐ DELL ☐ HP-COMPAQ ☐ IBM

☐ GATEWAY ☐ SONY ☐ TOSHIBA ☐ OTHER

3. **Approximately how long ago did you contact PC help-desk services?**

☐ Less than three months ago

☐ More than three months ago

☐ I do not remember

4. **Service-provider was willing to help me.**

Strongly   Strongly
Disagree   Agree

☐ 1   ☐ 2   ☐ 3   ☐ 4   ☐ 5   ☐ 6

5. Service-provider was courteous while providing responses.

Strongly   Strongly
Disagree   Agree

☐ 1   ☐ 2   ☐ 3   ☐ 4   ☐ 5   ☐ 6

6. My issues were resolved speedily.

Strongly   Strongly
Disagree   Agree

☐ 1   ☐ 2   ☐ 3   ☐ 4   ☐ 5   ☐ 6

7. Service-provider seemed to be technically competent.

Strongly   Strongly
Disagree   Agree

☐ 1   ☐ 2   ☐ 3   ☐ 4   ☐ 5   ☐ 6

8. Service-provider was readily available when I contacted the service number.

Strongly   Strongly
Disagree   Agree

☐ 1   ☐ 2   ☐ 3   ☐ 4   ☐ 5   ☐ 6

9. Service-provider spoke at a speed I could understand.

Strongly   Strongly
Disagree   Agree

☐ 1   ☐ 2   ☐ 3   ☐ 4   ☐ 5   ☐ 6

10. Service-provider spoke with a heavy foreign accent.

Strongly
Disagree

Strongly
Agree

☐ 1   ☐ 2   ☐ 3   ☐ 4   ☐ 5   ☐ 6

11. Service-provider's pronunciation was clear to me.

Strongly
Disagree

Strongly
Agree

☐ 1   ☐ 2   ☐ 3   ☐ 4   ☐ 5   ☐ 6

12. The instructions given by the service-provider were clear.

Strongly
Disagree

Strongly
Agree

☐ 1   ☐ 2   ☐ 3   ☐ 4   ☐ 5   ☐ 6

13. Service-provider spoke in fluent English.

Strongly
Disagree

Strongly
Agree

☐ 1   ☐ 2   ☐ 3   ☐ 4   ☐ 5   ☐ 6

14. Service-provider seemed to be struggling to find the right words.

Strongly
Disagree

Strongly
Agree

☐ 1   ☐ 2   ☐ 3   ☐ 4   ☐ 5   ☐ 6

15. Service-provider understood my issues clearly.

Strongly   Strongly
Disagree   Agree

☐ 1   ☐ 2   ☐ 3   ☐ 4   ☐ 5   ☐ 6

16. I was guided by the service-provider as I acted on his/her instructions.

Strongly   Strongly
Disagree   Agree

☐ 1   ☐ 2   ☐ 3   ☐ 4   ☐ 5   ☐ 6

17. Service-provider followed-up a few days later to ensure my issue was resolved.

Strongly   Strongly
Disagree   Agree

☐ 1   ☐ 2   ☐ 3   ☐ 4   ☐ 5   ☐ 6

18. Service-provider had a friendly attitude.

Strongly   Strongly
Disagree   Agree

☐ 1   ☐ 2   ☐ 3   ☐ 4   ☐ 5   ☐ 6

19. Service-provider was not sincere in his/her efforts to help me.

Strongly   Strongly
Disagree   Agree

☐ 1   ☐ 2   ☐ 3   ☐ 4   ☐ 5   ☐ 6

20. I felt cheated by the service-provider

Strongly   Strongly
Disagree   Agree

☐ 1   ☐ 2   ☐ 3   ☐ 4   ☐ 5   ☐ 6

21. Service-provider understood my urgency.

Strongly   Strongly
Disagree   Agree

☐ 1   ☐ 2   ☐ 3   ☐ 4   ☐ 5   ☐ 6

22. Service-provider listened to me patiently.

Strongly   Strongly
Disagree   Agree

☐ 1   ☐ 2   ☐ 3   ☐ 4   ☐ 5   ☐ 6

23. I could trust the service provider to solve my issue.

Strongly   Strongly
Disagree   Agree

☐ 1   ☐ 2   ☐ 3   ☐ 4   ☐ 5   ☐ 6

24. The information given to me was relevant in resolving my issue.

Strongly   Strongly
Disagree   Agree

☐ 1   ☐ 2   ☐ 3   ☐ 4   ☐ 5   ☐ 6

25. I could trust the service-provider to safeguard my personal information.

Strongly   Strongly
Disagree   Agree

☐ 1   ☐ 2   ☐ 3   ☐ 4   ☐ 5   ☐ 6

26. The service-provider was caring.

Strongly   Strongly
Disagree   Agree

☐ 1   ☐ 2   ☐ 3   ☐ 4   ☐ 5   ☐ 6

27. Overall, I was satisfied with help I received from service provider.

Strongly   Strongly
Disagree   Agree

☐ 1   ☐ 2   ☐ 3   ☐ 4   ☐ 5   ☐ 6

28. I think the service-provider was based in

☐ U.S.A   ☐ A FOREIGN COUNTRY

THANK YOU

You have reached the end of the survey. Your response has been recorded. We appreciate your participation. Thank you,

V. Sunder

University of Phoenix-School of Advanced Studies

APPENDIX E

CODING OF SPSS DATA

Original Question Number	SPSS Code	Question
	id	ID
1	Q3	Gender
2	Q4	Type of PC/laptop you called help-desk about
3	Q5	Approximately how long ago did you contact PC help-desk services?
4	Q6	PC/laptop Service-provider was willing to help me.
5	Q7	Service-provider was courteous while providing responses.
6	Q8	My issues were resolved speedily.
7	Q9	Service-provider seemed to be technically competent.
8	Q10	Service-provider was readily available when I contacted the service number.
9	Q11	Service-provider spoke at a speed I could understand.
10	Q12	Service-provider spoke with a heavy foreign accent.
11	Q13	Service-provider pronunciation was clear to me.
12	Q14	The instructions given by the service-provider were clear.
13	Q15	Service-provider spoke in fluent English.
14	Q16	Service-provider seemed to be struggling to find the right words.

15	Q17	Service-provider understood my issues clearly.
16	Q18	I was guided by the service-provider as I acted on his/her instructions.
17	Q19	Service-provider followed-up a few days later to ensure my issue was resolved.
18	Q20	Service-provider had a friendly attitude.
19	Q21	Service-provider was NOT sincere in his/her efforts to help me.
20	Q22	I felt cheated by the service-provider.
21	Q23	Service-provider understood my urgency.
22	Q24	Service-provider listened to me patiently.
23	Q25	I could trust the service provider to solve my issue.
24	Q26	The information given to me was relevant in resolving my issue.
25	Q27	I could trust the service-provider to safeguard my personal information.
26	Q28	The service-provider was caring.
27	Q29	Overall, I was satisfied with help I received from service provider.
28	Q30	I think the service-provider was based in USA A FOREIGN COUNTRY

APPENDIX F

DESCRIPTIVE STATISTICS WITH DESCENDING MEANS

Scale 1 (Strongly Disagree) to 6 (Strongly Agree)
With no intermediate labels

	Mean	Std. Dev.
Service-provider was courteous while providing responses.	4.974	1.111
PC/laptop service-provider was willing to help me.	4.873	1.230
I felt cheated by the service-provider.** (Interpret score as "I did not feel cheated by the service provider")	4.792	1.537
Service-provider was not sincere in his/her efforts to help me.** Interpret score as "Service-provider was sincere in his/her efforts to help me."	4.719	1.481
Service-provider listened to me patiently.	4.652	1.276
I was guided by the service-provider as I acted on his/her instructions.	4.639	1.249
I could trust the service-provider to safeguard my personal information.	4.588	1.192
Service-provider seemed to be technically competent.	4.547	1.342
Service-provider spoke at a speed I could understand.	4.423	1.444

Service-provider was readily available when I contacted the service number.	4.416	1.374
Service-provider understood my issues clearly.	4.303	1.425
Service-provider seemed to be struggling to find the right words. ** Interpret score as "Service-provider did not seem to be struggling to find the right words."	4.270	1.581
Service-provider understood my urgency.	4.268	1.441
Service-provider pronunciation was clear to me.	4.032	1.566
My issues were resolved speedily.	4.000	1.574
Service-provider spoke with a heavy foreign accent.	3.745	1.934
Service-provider followed-up a few days later to ensure my issue was resolved.	2.871	1.888

APPENDIX G

COMPARISON OF GROUPED MEANS

Question	I think the service-provider was based in	Mean
PC/laptop service-provider was willing to help me.	USA	5.030
	A foreign country	4.668
Service-provider was courteous while providing responses.	USA	5.129
	A foreign country	4.772
My issues were resolved speedily.	USA	4.424
	A foreign country	3.446
Service-provider seemed to be technically competent.	USA	4.886
	A foreign country	4.104
Service-provider was readily available when I contacted the service number.	USA	4.682
	A foreign country	4.069
Service-provider spoke at a speed I could understand.	USA	4.917
	A foreign country	3.777
Service-provider spoke with a heavy foreign accent.	USA	2.705
	A foreign country	5.104

Service-provider pronunciation was clear to me.	USA	4.795
	A foreign country	3.035
Service-provider seemed to be struggling to find the right words.	USA	4.625
	A foreign country	3.807
Service-provider understood my issues clearly.	USA	4.750
	A foreign country	3.718
I was guided by the service-provider as I acted on his/her instructions.	USA	4.830
	A foreign country	4.391
Service-provider followed-up a few days later to ensure my issue was resolved.	USA	3.235
	A foreign country	2.396
Service-provider was NOT sincere in his/her efforts to help me.	USA	4.875
	A foreign country	4.515
I felt cheated by the service-provider.	USA	5.008
	A foreign country	4.510
Service-provider understood my urgency.	USA	4.636
	A foreign country	3.787
Service-provider listened to me patiently.	USA	4.905
	A foreign country	4.322
I could trust the service-provider to safeguard my personal information.	USA	4.826
	A foreign country	4.277

APPENDIX H: RUN A

ROTATED COMPONENT MATRIX EIGENVALUES>1.00

	Component		
	A	B	C
	1	2	3
My issues were resolved speedily.	0.790	0.219	0.130
Service-provider seemed to be technically competent.	0.738	0.348	0.192
Service-provider understood my issues clearly.	0.696	0.277	0.376
Service-provider was readily available when I contacted the service number.	0.692	0.273	0.059
Service-provider understood my urgency.	0.679	0.250	0.282
I could trust the service-provider to safeguard my personal information.	0.658	0.222	0.127
Service-provider spoke at a speed I could understand.	0.654	0.214	0.443
Service-provider listened to me patiently.	0.596	0.529	0.232
Service-provider pronunciation was clear to me.	0.592	0.131	0.624

Service-provider followed-up a few days later to ensure my issue was resolved.	0.592	-0.126	-0.075
PC/laptop service-provider was willing to help me.	0.591	0.625	-0.054
Service-provider was courteous while providing responses.	0.589	0.599	-0.015
I was guided by the service-provider as I acted on his/her instructions.	0.547	0.543	0.125
I felt cheated by the service-provider.**	0.167	0.718	0.367
Service-provider was NOT sincere in his/her efforts to help me.**	0.092	0.821	0.275
Service-provider seemed to be struggling to find the right words.**	-0.038	0.433	0.718
Service-provider spoke with a heavy foreign accent.	-0.147	-0.075	-0.875

APPENDIX I

RUN A: EXPLAINED VARIANCE

Component	Initial Eigen-values			Rotation Sums of Squared Loadings		
	Total	% of Variance	Cumulative %	Total	% of Variance	Cumulative %
1	8.347	49.099	49.099	5.566	32.741	32.741
2	1.708	10.045	59.144	3.217	18.926	51.667
3	1.179	6.935	66.080	2.450	14.412	66.080
4	0.819	4.818	70.898			
5	0.694	4.084	74.982			
6	0.598	3.520	78.502			
7	0.561	3.301	81.803			
8	0.452	2.656	84.459			
9	0.415	2.444	86.902			
10	0.401	2.357	89.260			
11	0.374	2.200	91.460			
12	0.311	1.829	93.289			
13	0.303	1.782	95.071			
14	0.243	1.427	96.499			

15	0.214	1.258	97.757
16	0.195	1.148	98.905
17	0.186	1.095	100.000

Extraction Method: Principal Component Analysis.

APPENDIX J

RUN B: EXPLAINED VARIANCE

	Total Variance Explained					
	Initial Eigenvalues			Rotation Sums of Squared Loadings		
	Total	% of Variance	Cumulative %	Total	% of Variance	Cumulative %
1	8.347	49.099	49.099	2.825	16.616	16.616
2	1.708	10.045	59.144	2.689	15.817	32.434
3	1.179	6.935	66.080	2.177	12.803	45.237
4	0.819	4.818	70.898	2.107	12.396	57.633
5	0.694	4.084	74.982	1.986	11.684	69.317
6	0.598	3.520	78.502	1.125	6.617	75.935
7	0.561	3.301	81.803	0.998	5.868	81.803
8	0.452	2.656	84.459			
9	0.415	2.444	86.902			
10	0.401	2.357	89.260			
11	0.374	2.200	91.460			
12	0.311	1.829	93.289			

13	0.303	1.782	95.071
14	0.243	1.427	96.499
15	0.214	1.258	97.757
16	0.195	1.148	98.905
17	0.186	1.095	100.000

Extraction Method: Principal Component Analysis.

APPENDIX K

REGRESSIONS BASED ON PERCEIVED SOURCES

	Foreign based	B	STD. Error	t	Sig.
(Constant)		4.399	0.082	53.544	0.000
FC 1	Clarity of issue	0.841	0.061	13.800	0.000
FC 5	Sincerity	0.634	0.073	8.648	0.000
FC 3	Technical dependability	0.611	0.055	11.049	0.000
FC 4	Quality of communication	0.465	0.079	5.890	0.000
FC 2	Compassionate responsiveness	0.448	0.060	7.497	0.000
FC 7	Trust	0.295	0.053	5.606	0.000
FC 6	Follow-up	0.320	0.062	5.121	0.000

	US based	B	Std. Error	t	Sig.
(Constant)		4.501	0.056	80.194	0.000
FC 1	Clarity of issue	0.772	0.051	15.256	0.000
FC 5	Sincerity	0.522	0.041	12.800	0.000
FC 2	Compassionate responsiveness	0.508	0.044	11.658	0.000
FC 3	Technical dependability	0.507	0.051	10.000	0.000
FC 7	Trust	0.288	0.049	5.850	0.000
FC 6	Follow-up	0.259	0.047	5.542	0.000
FC 4	Quality of communication	0.207	0.054	3.820	0.000

APPENDIX L

MEAN DIFFERENCES OF SCALE SCORES

	ID	Mean Differences (US-Foreign)	t*
Service-provider pronunciation was clear to me.	Q13	1.761	14.475
Service-provider spoke at a speed I could understand.	Q11	1.139	9.163
Service-provider understood my issues clearly.	Q17	1.032	8.294
My issues were resolved speedily.	Q8	0.979	6.985
Service-provider understood my urgency.	Q23	0.849	6.586
Service-provider followed-up a few days later to ensure my issue was resolved.	Q19	0.839	4.866
Service-provider seemed to be struggling to find the right words.	Q16	0.818	5.722
Service-provider seemed to be technically competent.	Q9	0.782	6.508
Service-provider was readily available when I contacted the service number.	Q10	0.613	4.886
Service-provider listened to me patiently.	Q24	0.584	5.016

I could trust the service-provider to safeguard my personal information.	Q27	0.549	5.050
I felt cheated by the service-provider.	Q22	0.498	3.505
I was guided by the service-provider as I acted on his/her instructions.	Q18	0.438	3.809
PC/laptop service-provider was willing to help me.	Q6	0.362	3.179
Service-provider was NOT sincere in his/her efforts to help me.	Q21	0.360	2.617
Service-provider was courteous while providing responses.	Q7	0.357	3.474
Service-provider spoke with a heavy foreign accent.	Q12	-2.399	-16.826

* df=464 for all t-tests in this table. All values of p were <0.01

REFERENCES

Aga, M., and Safakli, O. V. (2007). An empirical investigation of service quality and customer satisfaction in professional accounting firms: evidence from North Cyprus. *Problems and Perspectives in Management, 4*(3), 21-29.

Aggarwal, P., Castleberry, S. B., Shepherd, C. D., and Ridnour, R. (2005). Salesperson empathy and listening: Impact on relationship outcomes. *Journal of Marketing Theory and Practice, 13*(3), 16-31.

Agustin, C., and Singh, J. (2005). Curvilinear effects of consumer loyalty determinants in relational exchanges. *Journal of Marketing Research, 42*(1), 96-108.

Ahearne, M., Mathieu, J., and Rapp, A. (2005). To empower or not to empower your sales force? An empirical examination of the influence of leadership empowerment behavior on customer satisfaction and performance. *Journal of Applied Psychology, 90*(5), 945-955.

Allen, D. R., and Rao, T. R. (2000). *Analysis of customer satisfaction data.* Milwaukee, WI: ASQ Quality Press.

Alster, N. (2005, Fall). Customer disservice. *CFO-IT, 23,* 1-16.

Andersen, P. A., and Blackburn, T. R. (2004). An experimental study of language intensity and response rate in Internet surveys. *Communication Reports, 17*(2), 73-84.

Anderson, E. W., Fornell, C., and Mazvancheryl, S. (2004). Customer satisfaction and shareholder value. *Journal of Marketing, 68*(4), 172-185.

Athanassopoulos, A. D., and Iliakopoulos, A. (2003). Modeling customer satisfaction in telecommunications: Assessing the effects of multiple transaction points on the perceived overall performance of the provider. *Production and Operations Management, 12*(2), 550-552.

Bailey, J. (2006). Profile on Theodore Levitt: The father of modern marketing. *Engineering Management, 16*(5), 48-49.

Barger, P. B., and Grandey, A. A. (2006). Service with a smile and encounter satisfaction: emotional contagion and appraisal mechanisms. *Academy of Management Journal, 49,* 1220-1238.

Barsky, J., and Nash, L. (2003). Customer satisfaction: Applying concepts to industry-wide measures. *Cornell Hotel and Restaurant Administration Quarterly, 44*(5/6).

Barthelemy, J. (2003). The seven deadly sins of outsourcing. *Academy of Management Executive, 17,* 387-412.

Bartikowski, B., Barthelemy, J., and Llosa, S. (2004). Customer satisfaction measurement: comparing four methods of attribute categorisations. *Service Industries Journal, 24*(4), 12-19.

Bauer H. H., Falk, T., and Hammerschmidt, M. (2006). eTransQual: A transaction process-based approach for capturing service quality in online shopping, *Journal of Business Research, 59,* 866-875.

Beatson, A., Lee, N., and Coote, L. V. (2007). Self-service technology and the service encounter. *Service Industries Journal, 27*(1), 75-89.

Beaujean, M., Davidson, J., and Madge, S. (2006). The "moment of truth" in customer service. *McKinsey Quarterly* (1), 62-73.

Beier, K., Woratschek, H., and Zieschang, K. (2004). The importance of sports in tourism: measurement of the customer satisfaction by the ISL approach. *Journal of Sport Tourism, 9*(2), 208-212.

Bennington, L., Cummane, J., and Conn, P. (2000). Customer satisfaction and call centers: An Australian study. *International Journal of Service Industry Management, 11*(2), 89-105.

Beshouri, C. P., Farrell, D., and Umezawa, F. (2005). Attracting more offshoring to the Philippines. *McKinsey Quarterly* (4), 12-15.

Bitner, M. J. (1990). Evaluating service encounters: The effects of physical surroundings and employee responses. *Journal of Marketing, 54*(2), 69-82.

Bharadwaj, N., and Roggeveen, A.L. (2008). The impact of off-shored and outsourced call service centers on customer appraisals. *Marketing Letters, 19*(1), 1-13.

Boshoff, C., and Staude, G. (2003). Satisfaction with service recovery: Its measurement and its outcomes. *South African Journal of Business Management, 34*(3), 9-18.

Brooks, N. (2006). Understanding IT outsourcing and its potential effects on IT workers and their environment. *Journal of Computer Information Systems, 46*(4), 46-53.

Buda, R., Sengupta, K., and Elsayed-Elkhouly, S. (2006). Employee and organizational perspectives of service quality: A cross-cultural study in Kuwait, United States, and Saudi Arabia. *International Journal of Management, 23*(3), 12-17.

Burns, R. C., Graefe, A. R., and Absher, J. D. (2003). Alternate **measurement** approaches to recreational **customer satisfaction: satisfaction**-only versus gap scores. *Leisure Sciences, 25*(4), 1-18.

Buttle, F. (1996). SERVQUAL: Review, critique, research agenda. *European Journal of Marketing, 30*(1), 8-32.

Chan, W. M., and Ibrahim, R. N. (2004). Evaluating the quality level of a product with multiple quality characteristics. *International Journal of Advanced Manufacturing Technology, 24*, 738-742.

Chandrashekaran, M., Rotte, K., Tax, S. S., and Grewal, R. (2007). Satisfaction strength and customer loyalty. *Journal of Marketing Research, 44*(1), 153-163.

Chang, L. (1994). A psychometric evaluation of 4-point and 6-point Likert-type scales in relation to reliability and validity. *Applied Psychological Measurement, 18*, 205-215.

Chatterjee, S., and Chatterjee, A. (2005). Prioritization of service quality parameters based on ordinal responses. *Total Quality Management and Business Excellence, 16*. 477-489.

Chen, K. (2005). Technology-based service and customer satisfaction in developing countries. *International Journal of Management, 22*, 307-319.

Chen, T., and Lee, Y. (2006). Kano two-dimensional quality model and important-performance analysis in the student's dormitory service quality evaluation in Taiwan. *Journal of American Academy of Business Cambridge, 9*(2), 33-38.

Chiu, H., and Lin, N. (2004). A service quality measurement derived from the theory of needs. *The Service Industries Journal, 24*(1), 187-204.

Chun, R. (2005). Corporate reputation: Meaning and measurement. *International Journal of Management Reviews, 7*(2), 91-109.

Clason, D. L., and Dormody, T. J. (1994). Analyzing data measured by individual Likert-type items. *Journal of Agricultural Education, 35*(4), 31-35.

Coelho, P. S., and Esteves, S.P. (2007). The choice between a five-point and a ten-point scale in the framework of customer satisfaction measurement. *International Journal of Market Research, 49*, 313-340.

Cooil, B., Keiningham, T. L., Aksoy, L., and Hsu, M. (2007). A longitudinal analysis of customer satisfaction and share of wallet: investigating the moderating effect of customer characteristics. *Journal of Marketing,* *71*(1), 67-83.

Costa, G., Glinia, E., Goudas, M., and Panagiotis, A. (2004). Recreational services in resort hotels: customer satisfaction aspects. *Journal of Sport Tourism, 9*(2), 17-21.

Crie, D. (2003). Consumers' complaint behavior, taxonomy, typology, and determinants: Towards a unified ontology. *Journal of Database Marketing and Customer Strategy Management, 11*(1), 1448-1551.

Cronin, J. J., and Taylor, S. A. (1992). Measuring service quality: a reexamination and extension. *Journal of Marketing, 56*(3), 55-68.

Cunningham, L. F., Young, C. E., and Lee, M. (2002). Cross-cultural perspectives of service quality and risk in air transportation. *Journal of Air Transportation, 7*(1), 10-25.

Dawes, J. (2008).Do data characteristics change according to the number of scale points used? *International Journal of Market Research, 50*(1), 25-32.

Deloitte Touché LLP. (2005). *Calling a change in the outsourcing market: The realities for the world's largest organizations.* Retrieved December 10, 2007, from http://www.deloitte.com/dtt/cda/doc/content/us_outsourcing_callingachange.pdf.

De Toni, A., and Tonchia, S. (2004). Measuring and managing after-sales service: Aprilia's experience. *International Journal of Services Technology and Management, 5,385-393.*

Doh, J. P. (2005). Offshore outsourcing: implications for international business and strategic management theory and practice. *Journal of Management Studies, 42,* 695-704.

Douglas, T., and Fredendall, L. D. (2004). Evaluating the Deming management model of total quality in services. *Decision Sciences, 35,* 393-422.

Durvasula, S., Lobo, A. C., Lysonski, S., and Mehta, S. C. (2006). Finding the sweet spot: a two-industry study using the zone of tolerance to identify determinant service quality attributes. *Journal of Financial Services Marketing, 10*(3), 173-194.

Edmondson, A. C., and McManus, S. E. (2007). Methodological fit in management field research. *Academy of Management Review, 32,* 1155-1174.

Economidou-Kogetsidis, M. (2005). "Yes, tell me please, what time is the midday flight from Athens arriving?": Telephone service encounters and politeness. *Intercultural Pragmatics, 2,* 253-274.

Fairell, D., Kaka, N, and Stürze, S. (2005). Ensuring India's offshoring future. *McKinsey Quarterly,* 2005 Special Edition.

Farnell, C. (2008). *ACSI quarterly commentaries Q2.* Retrieved November 20, 2008, from http://www.theacsi.org.

Field, A.P. (2005). *Discovering statistics using SPSS* (2nd ed.). London: Sage.

Fox-Wasylyshyn, S. M., and El-Masri, M. M. (2005). Handling missing data in self-report measures. *Research in Nursing and Health, 28,* 488-495.

Froehle, C. M. (2006). Service personnel, technology, and their interaction in influencing customer satisfaction. *Decision Sciences, 37*(1), 5-38.

Garbarino, E., and Johnson, M. S. (1999). The different roles of satisfaction, trust, and commitment in customer relationships. *Journal of Marketing, 63*(2), 70-87.

Gardner, H. J., and Martin, M. A. (2007). Analyzing ordinal scales in studies of virtual environments. *Presence-Massachusetts Institute of Technology, 16,* 447-455.

George, D., and Mallery, P. (2003). *SPSS for Windows step by step: a simple guide and reference. 11.0 update* (4th ed.). Boston: Allyn and Bacon.

Gliem, J. R., and Gliem, R. R. (2003). *Calculating, interpreting, and reporting Cronbach's alpha reliability coefficient for Likert-type scales.* Paper presented at the 2003 Midwest Research to Practice Conference in Adult, Continuing, and Community education.

Goode, M. M. H., Davies, F., **Moutinho, L., and** Jamal, A. (2005). Determining customer satisfaction from mobile phones: A neural network approach. *Journal of Marketing Management, 21* (7/8), 43-51.

Gottfredson, M., Puryear, R., and Phillips, S. (2005). Strategic sourcing from periphery to the core. *Harvard Business Review, 83,* 312-339.

Griffiths, K. (2006). Got satisfaction? *Industrial Distribution, 95,* 312-317.

Gruca, T. S., and Rego, L. L. (2005). Customer satisfaction, cash flow, and shareholder value. *Journal of Marketing, 69*(3), 115-130.

Gupta, S., and Zeithaml, V. (2006). Customer metrics and their impact on financial performance. *Marketing Science, 25,* 718-739.

Hong, S. Y. J., and Goo, J. (2004). A causal model of customer loyalty in professional service firms: An empirical study. *International Journal of Management, 21,* 243-260.

Horn, D., Feinberg, R., and Salvendy, G. (2005). Determinant elements of customer relationship management in e-business. *Behavior and Information Technology, 24* (2), 101-110.

Hsiu-Fen, L. (2007). The impact of website quality dimensions on customer satisfaction in the B2C e-commerce context. *Total Quality Management and Business Excellence, 18* (4), 119-138.

Israel, G. D. (2003). *Determining sample size.* Gainesville: University of Florida, IFAS Extension.

Jain, S. K., and Gupta, G. (2004). Measuring service quality: SERVQUAL vs. SERVPERF Scales. *Vikalpa: The Journal for Decision Makers, 29*(2), 25-37.

Jamieson, S. (2004). **Likert scales:** How to (ab) use them. *Medical Education, 38*(12), 53-61.

Jeyapaul, R., Shahabudeen, P., and Krishnaiah, K. (2005). Quality management research by considering multiresponse problems in the **Taguchi** method—A review. *International Journal of Advanced Manufacturing Technology, 26*(11/12), 64-72.

Jianan, W., and DeSarbo, W. S. (2005). Market segmentation for customer satisfaction studies via a new latent structure multidimensional scaling model. *Applied Stochastic Models in Business and Industry, 21*(4/5), 32-43.

Johns, N., Avci, T., and Karatepe, O. M. (2004). Measuring service quality of travel agents: Evidence from northern Cyprus. *Service Industries Journal, 24*(3), 82-100.

Johnson, M. S., Garbarino, E., and Sivadas, E. (2006). Influences of customer differences of loyalty, perceived risk, and category experience on customer satisfaction ratings. *International Journal of Market Research, 48,* 441-445.

Jones, D. L., Mak, B., and Sim, J. (2007). A new look at the antecedents and consequences of relationship quality in the hotel service environment. *Services Marketing Quarterly, 28*(3), 15-31.

Jones, M. T. (2005). The transnational corporation, corporate social responsibility, and the outsourcing debate. *Journal of American Academy of Business Cambridge, 6,* 509-521.

Kettinger, W. J., and Lee, C. C. (2005). Zones of tolerance: Alternative scales for measuring information systems service quality. *MIS Quarterly, 29,* 606-621.

Kocakoç, I. D., and Sen, A. (2006). Utilising surveys for finding improvement areas for customer satisfaction along the supply chain. *International Journal of Market Research, 48*(5), 102-115.

Koh, C., Ang, S., and Straub, D. W. (2004). IT outsourcing success: A psychological contract perspective. *Information Systems Research, 15,* 356-373.

Koprovski, G. J. (2006). Apple leads all other PC makers in customer satisfaction by default. *Macnewsworld.* Retrieved December 17, 2006, from http://www. macnewsworld.com/story/52569.html.

Kosciulek, J. E. (2003). A multidimensional approach to the structure of consumer **satisfaction** with vocational rehabilitation services. *Rehabilitation Counseling Bulletin, 46*(2), 92-97.

Kouthouris, C., and Alexandris, K. (2005). Can service quality predict customer satisfaction and behavioral intentions in the sport tourism industry? An application of the SERVQUAL model in an outdoors setting. *Journal of Sport Tourism, 10*(2), 101-110.

Krampf, R., Ueltschy, L., and D'Amico, M. (2003). The contribution of emotion to consumer satisfaction in the service setting. *Marketing Management Journal, 13*(1), 32-52.

Kuo, T., Lu, I., Huang, C., and Wu, G. (2005). Measuring users' perceived portal service quality: An empirical study. *Total Quality Management and Business Excellence, 16,* 309-320.

Kuo, Y. (2004). Integrating Kano's model into Web—Community service quality. *Total Quality Management and Business Excellence, 15,* 925-939.

Laroche, M., Ueltschy, L. C., Abe, S., Cleveland, M., and Yannopoulos, P. P. (2004). Service quality perceptions and customer satisfaction: Evaluating the role of culture. *Journal of International Marketing, 12*(3), 58-85.

Lee, L. (2006). **Dell: Facing up to past mistakes.** *Business Week,* (3989), 1-4.

Lee, M. C., and Hwan, I. S. (2005). Relationships among service quality, customer satisfaction, and profitability in the Taiwanese banking industry. *International Journal of Management, 22,* 535-648.

Liao, Z., and Cheung, T. M. (2008). Measuring consumer satisfaction in internet banking: A core framework. *Communications of the ACM, 51,* 248-250.

Liao, H. (2003). Using PCR-TOPSIS to optimise **Taguchi's** multiresponse problem. *International Journal of Advanced Manufacturing Technology, 22,* 649-655.

Liu, C. (2005). The multidimensional and hierarchical structure of perceived quality and customer satisfaction. *International Journal of Management, 22,* 261-273.

Lubke, G. H., and Muthén, B. H. (2004). Applying multigroup confirmatory factor models for continuous outcomes to Likert scale data complicates meaningful group comparisons. *Structural Equation Modeling, 11*(4), 125-136.

Luo, X., and Bhattacharya, C. B. (2006). Corporate social responsibility, customer satisfaction, and market value. *Journal of Marketing, 70*(4), 1-18.

Luo, X., and Homburg, C. (2007). Neglected outcomes of customer satisfaction. *Journal of Marketing, 71*(2), 34-39.

Malhotra, N. K., Ulgado, F. M., Agarwal, J., Shainesh, G., and Wu, L. (2005). Dimensions of service quality in developed and developing economies: Multicountry cross-cultural *International Marketing Review, 22*(3), 256-278.

Marley, K. A., **Collier,** D. A., and **Goldstein,** S. M. (2004). The role of clinical and process quality in achieving patient satisfaction in hospitals. *Decision Sciences, 35*(3), 349-369.

Marshall, J., and **Heffes,** E. M. (2005). Study: Many firms question benefits. *Financial Executive, 21*(5), 10-10.

Martinez-Tur, V., Peir, J. M., Ramos, J., and Moliner, C. (2006). Justice perceptions as predictors of customer satisfaction: The impact of distributive, procedural, and interactional Justice. *Journal of Applied Social Psychology, 36*(1), 100-119.

Massad, N., Heckman, R., and Crowston, K. (2006). Customer satisfaction with electronic service encounters. *International Journal of Electronic Commerce, 10*(4), 73-104.

Matsuura, H., Chiba, R., and Fujieda, M. (1999). Intelligibility and comprehensibility of American and Irish Englishes in Japan. *World Englishes, 18*(1), 49-62.

Mattila, A. S., and Mount, D. J. (2006). The impact of timeliness on complaint satisfaction in the context of call-centers. *Journal of Hospitality and Leisure Marketing, 14*(3), 5-16.

Matzler, K., Fuchs, M., and Schubert, A. K. (2004). Employee satisfaction: Does Kano's model apply? *Total Quality Management and Business Excellence, 15*(9/10), 1179-1198.

Matzler, K., Sauerwein, E., and Heischmidt, K. A. (2003). Importance-performance analysis revisited: The role of the factor structure of customer satisfaction. *Service Industries Journal, 23*(2), 112-129.

McConkey, C., W., Stevens, R. E., and Loudon, D. L. (2003). Surveying the service sector: A pilot study of the effectiveness of mail vs. Internet approaches. *Services Marketing Quarterly, 25*(1), 75-84.

Mello Jr., J. P. (2007). PC call centers provide dismal service. *CRM Buyer on-line*. Retrieved June 20, 2007, from http://www.crmbuyer.com/story/57798.html.

Meyer, C. and Schwager, A. (2007). Understanding customer experience. *Harvard Business Review, 85*(2), 116-126.

Michel, S. (2004). Consequences of perceived acceptability of a bank's service failures. *Journal of Financial Services Marketing, 8*(4), 367-377.

Morwitz, V. G. (2005). The effect of survey measurement on respondent behaviour. *Applied Stochastic Models in Business and Industry, 21*(4/5), 451-455.

Mukherjee, A., and Nath, P. (2005). An empirical assessment of comparative approaches to service quality measurement. *Journal of Services Marketing, 19*(3), 174-184.

Neuman, W. L. (2003). *Social Research Methods*. Boston, MA: Allyn and Bacon.

Nicholls, M. E. R., Orr, C. A., Okubo, M, and Loftus, A. (2006). Satisfaction guaranteed: The effect of spatial biases on responses to Likert scales. *Psychological Science, 17*(12), 1027-1028.

Oliver, R. L. (1980). A cognitive model of the antecedents and consequences of satisfaction decisions. *Journal of Marketing Research, 17*(4), 460-469.

Oliver, R. L. (1997). *Satisfaction: A behavioral perspective in the consumer.* New York: McGraw-Hill.

Oliver, R. L., and Rust, R. T. (1997). Customer delight: Foundations, findings, and managerial insight. *Journal of Retailing, 73*(3), 311-336.

Olsen, S. O., Wilcox, J., and Olsson, U. (2005). Consequences of ambivalence on satisfaction and loyalty. *Psychology and Marketing, 22*(3), 247-269.

O'Rourke, T. W. (2003). Methodological techniques for dealing with missing data. *American Journal of Health Studies, 18*(2/3), 165-168.

Owuor, C. O., and Zumbo, B.D. (2001). *Implications of ordinal scale categorization on regression models under different distributions and conditions: An assessment of the accuracy and information of Likert scales on regression analysis.* Paper presented at the NCME Conference University of British Columbia, Seattle, WA. Retrieved from www.educ.ubc.ca/faculty/zumbo/ins2001/index.html.

Panther, T., and Farquhar, J. D. (2004). Consumer responses to dissatisfaction with financial service providers: An exploration of why some stay while others switch. *Journal of Financial Services Marketing, 8*(4), 343-353.

Parasuraman, A., Zeithaml, V. A., and Berry, L. L. (1988). SERVQUAL: A multiple item scale for measuring consumer perceptions of service quality. *Journal of Retailing, 64*(1), 5-6.

Parasuraman, A., Zeithaml, V.A., and Malhotra, A. (2005). E-S-QUAL: A multiple-item scale for assessing electronic service quality. *Journal of Service Research, 7*(3), 213-233.

Payne, A., and Frow, P. (2005). A strategic framework for customer relationship management. *Journal of Marketing, 69*(4), 167-176.

Pett, M. A., Lackey, N. R., and Sullivan, J. J. (2003). *Making sense of factor analysis: The use of factor analysis for instrument development in health care research.* Thousand Oaks, CA: Sage.

Piligrimienė, Ž., and Bučiūnienė, I. (2008). Different perspectives on health care quality: Is the consensus possible? *Engineering Economics, 56*(1), 104-111.

Preston, C. C., and Colman, A. (2000). Optimal number of response categories in rating scales: reliability, validity, discriminating power, and respondent preferences. *Acta Psychologica, 104,* 1-15.

Radclifte, N. J., and Simpson, R. (2008). Identifying who can be saved and who will be driven away by retention activity. *Journal of Telecommunications Management, 1*(2), 168-176.

Raghuram, S. (2006). Individual effectiveness in outsourcing. *Human Systems Management, 25*(2), 127-133.

Raghunathan, T. E. (2004). What do we do with missing data? Some options for analysis of incomplete data. *Annual Review of Public Health, 25*(1), 99-117.

Ranaweera, C. (2007). Are satisfied long-term customers more profitable? Evidence from the telecommunication sector. *Journal of Targeting, Measurement and Analysis for Marketing, 15*(2), 113-120.

Ranaweera, C., and Prabhu, J. (2003). On the relative importance of customer satisfaction and trust as determinants of customer retention and positive word of mouth. *Journal of Targeting, Measurement and Analysis for Marketing, 12*(1), 82-90.

Roberts, M. L., Liu, R. R., and Hazard, K. (2005). Strategy, technology, and organisational alignment: Key components of CRM success. *Journal of Database Marketing and Customer Strategy Management, 12*(4), 315-326.

Roman, S. (2007). The ethics of online retailing: A scale development and validation from the consumers' perspective. *Journal of Business Ethics, 72*(2), 131-148.

Roscino, A., and Pollice, A. (2004). A statistical analysis of the customer satisfaction with car dealers. *Applied Stochastic Models in Business and Industry, 20*(3), 281-289.

Rubio, D. M., Berg-Weger, M., Tebb, S. S., Lee, E. S., and Rauch, S. (2003). **Objectifying content validity**: Conducting a **content validity** study in social work research. *Social Work Research, 27*(2), 94-104.

Saravanan, R., and Rao, K. S. P. (2007). Measurement of service quality from the customer's perspective—An empirical study. *Total Quality Management and Business Excellence, 18*(4), 435-449.

Saunders, J. A., Morrow-Howell, N., Spitznagel, E., Doré P., Proctor E. K., and Pescarino. R. (2006). Imputing missing data: A comparison of methods for social work researchers. *Social Work Research, 30*(1), 19-31.

Schniederjans, M. J., and Cao, Q. (2006). Strategic and tactical perception differences of outsourcing goal achievement: An empirical study. *Journal of Information Technology Management, 17*(1), 1-13.

Schultz, C. W. (2006). To offshore or not to offshore: which nations will win a disproportionate share of the economic value generated from the globalization of white-collar jobs? *Houston Journal of International Law, 29*(1), 231-269.

Scott, M. (2007). Luring customers with local call centers. *Business week online*. Retrieved August 15, 2007, from EBSCOhost database. ~~database.~~

Sele, K. (2006). Marketing ethics in emerging markets: Coping with ethical dilemmas. *IIMB Management Review, 18*(1), 95-104.

Shah, J. R., and Murtaza, M. B. (2005). Effective customer relationship management through web services. *Journal of Computer Information Systems, 46*(1), 98-109.

Sharma, N., and Ojha, S. (2004) Measuring service performance in mobile communications. *Service Industries Journal, 24*(6), 109-128.

Smith, A. M. (1995). Measuring service quality: Is SERVQUAL now redundant? *Journal of Marketing Management, 11*(1/3), 257-276.

Smith, R. E., and Wright, W. (2004). Determinants of customer loyalty and financial performance. *Journal of Management Accounting Research, 16*, 183-205.

Söderlund, M., and Julander, C. (2003). The variable nature of services: an empirical examination of trust and its effects on customers' satisfaction responses to poor and good service. *Total Quality Management and Business Excellence, 14*(3), 291-304.

Sturdy, A., and Fleming, P. (2003). Talk as technique—A critique of the words and deeds distinction in the diffusion of customer service cultures in call centres. *Journal of Management Studies, 40*(4), 753-773.

Sureshchandar, G. S., Rajendran, C., and Kamalanabhan, T. J. (2001). Customer perceptions of service quality: A critique. *Total Quality Management, 12*(1), 111-124.

Suuroja, M. (2003). *Service quality--main conceptualizations and critique.* (Working Paper Series No. 23). Tartu, Estonia: University of Tartu—Faculty of Economics and Business Administration, 3-27.

Swain, S. D., Weathers, D., and Niedrich, R. W. (2008). Assessing three sources of misresponse to reversed Likert items. *Journal of Marketing Research, 45*(1), 116-131.

Tam, J. M. (2004). Customer satisfaction, service quality, and perceived value: An integrative model. *Journal of Marketing Management, 20*(7/8), 897-917.

Taylor, T. (2005). In defense of outsourcing. *Cato Journal, 25*(2), 367-377.

The Research Advisors (TRA). (2008). *Sample size table.* Retrieved June 10, 2008, from http://www.research-advisors.com/tools/SampleSize. htm. van Dyke, T. P., Kappelman, L. A., and Prybutok, V. R. (1997). Measuring information systems service quality: Concerns on the use of the SERVQUAL questionnaire. *MIS Quarterly, 21*(2), 195-208.

Wegge, J., Vogt, J., and Wecking, C. (2007). Customer-induced stress in call centre work: A comparison of audio—and videoconference. *Journal of Occupational and Organizational Psychology, 80*(4), 693-712.

Wells, R. M. J. (2007). Outstanding customer satisfaction: The key to a talented workforce? *Academy of Management Perspectives, 21*(3), 87-89.

Winsted, K. F. (2000). Service behaviors that lead to satisfied customers. *European Journal of Marketing, 34*(3/4), 399-417.

Yang, C. (2005). The refined Kano's model and its application. *Total Quality Management and Business Excellence, 16*(10), 1127-1137.

Yeung, M. H., and Ennew, C. T. (2000). From customer satisfaction to profitability. *Journal of Strategic Marketing, 8*(4), 313-326.

Yu, S. (2007). An empirical investigation on the economic consequences of customer satisfaction. *Total Quality Management and Business Excellence, 18*(5), 555-569.

Zeithaml, V. A., and Bitner, M. J. (2003). *Services marketing: Integrating customer focus across the firm.* New York: McGraw-Hill.

Zodpey, S. P. (2004). Sample size and power analysis in medical research. *Indian Journal of Dermatology, Venereology and Leprology, 70*(2), 123-128.

Zulganef, G. M. (2006). The existence of overall satisfaction in service customer relationships *International Journal of Business, 8*(3), 301-321.

SUMMARY

Outsourcing of services to low-cost providers overseas has grown significantly in recent years. However, US customers have expressed dissatisfaction with some of the outsourced IT services, resulting in serious financial implications to businesses. This quantitative research study sought to find the determinants of customer satisfaction of outsourced help-desk services in the PC industry.

Based on a survey of 466 PC users in the United States, a new framework of customer satisfaction was developed with seven determinants:

Compassionate responsiveness
Sincerity
Clarity of issue
Technical dependability
Trust
Follow-up
Quality of communication.

Training of help-desk service providers in attitudinal, technical, and communication competencies based on these seven determinants has been recommended for improving customer satisfaction, thereby, benefiting firms and their stakeholders.

*   *   *

INDEX

www.ingramcontent.com/pod-product-compliance
Lightning Source LLC
Chambersburg PA
CBHW051240050326
40689CB00007B/1007